MURRAY L. PETERS

WHOOP'S APOSTROPHE...! #2

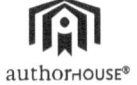

authorHOUSE®

AuthorHouse™ UK Ltd.
1663 Liberty Drive
Bloomington, IN 47403 USA
www.authorhouse.co.uk
Phone: 0800.197.4150

Published by AuthorHouse 7/17/2013

ISBN: 978-1-4918-0017-1 (sc)
ISBN: 978-1-4918-0032-4 (hc)
ISBN: 978-1-4918-0056-0 (e)

Dedicated to

the wonderful Iain Banks / Iain M. Banks – a kinder, wittier, more cool author I've yet to meet – he was also a damn fine writer of both Fiction and SF! ☹ (Hope you liked apostrophes Mr. B!).

TABLE OF CONTENTS

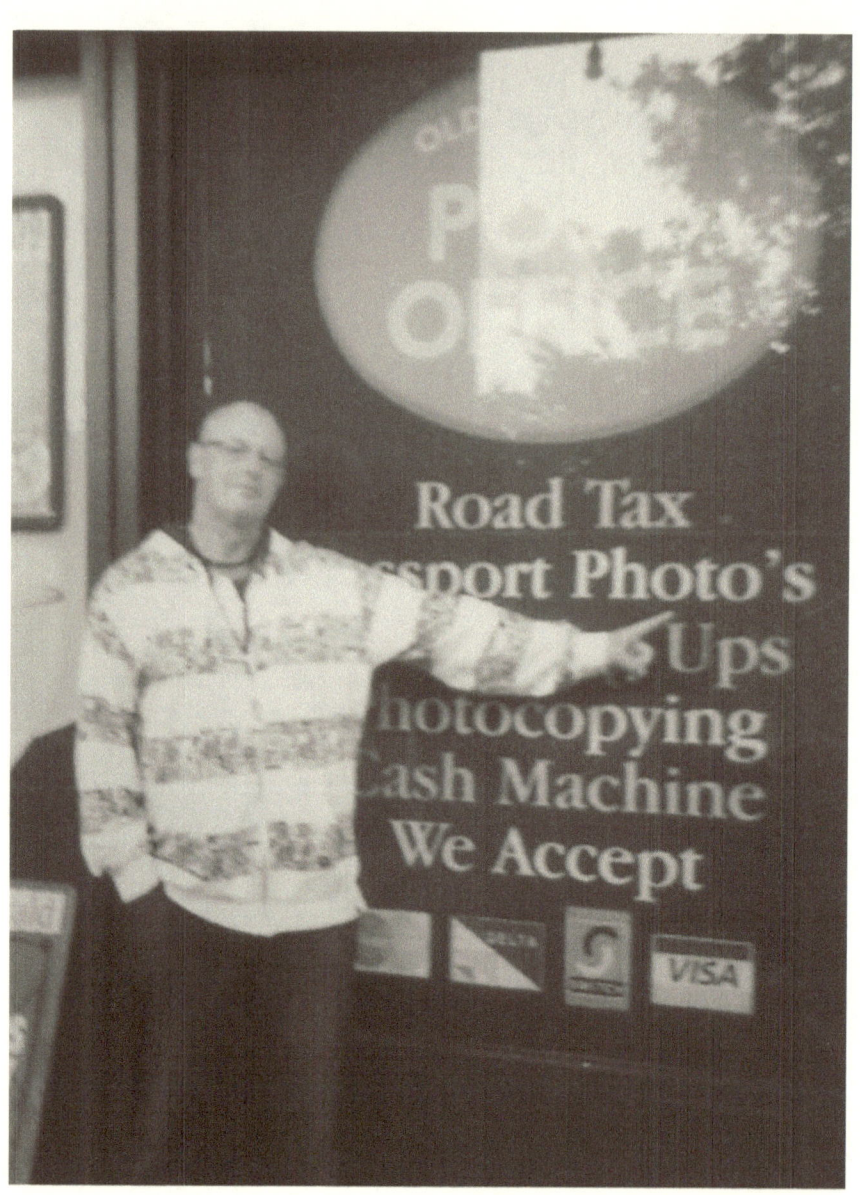

INTRODUCTION

Hi again,

Hope that you've enjoyed my "WHOOP'S APOSTROPHE...!" #1, because here's #2...another 100 crazy photographs of mad apostrophe (and spelling) errors from around the globe, fae Bonnie Scotland all the way 'Doon Under' to Australia!

Funny they are...horrid also, as the poor English teacher in me captures the error...but with a fair-sized (and apostrophe-shaped) lump in my throat! Enjoy!

THE HUMOUR IS IN THE HORROR!

MLP June 2013

P.S. Read Matt Engels' "I demand an end to the apostrophe" piece in 'The Guardian' 6/6/2000 - enjoy, laugh; smile at the "Greengrocers' Apostrophe" bit...but disagree! Please! ☺

(Read any of MLP's own 'Sci-fi' fiction in his ongoing "Boyle-Breath" Series yet? Number 3, "BOYLE-BREATH BEGINS BACK at the END" is out very soon! ("Boyle-Breath" and "Boyle-Breath Breathes" its sequel, lie smelling in wait for you now at authorhouse.com).

mlp.com for more info

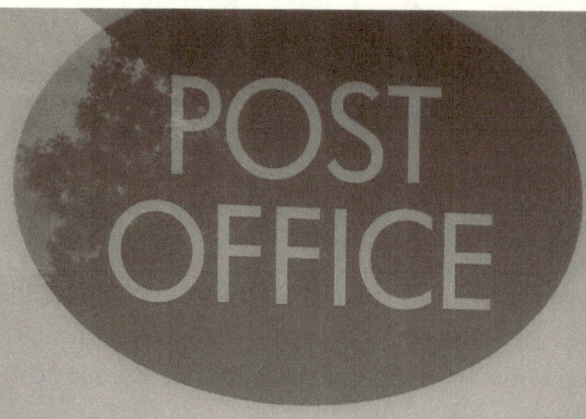

POST OFFICE

Road Tax
Passport Photos
Phone Top-Ups
Photocopying
Free Cash Machine
We Accept

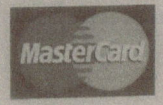 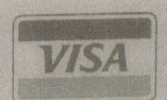 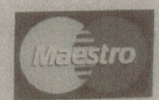

X

APOSTROPHES

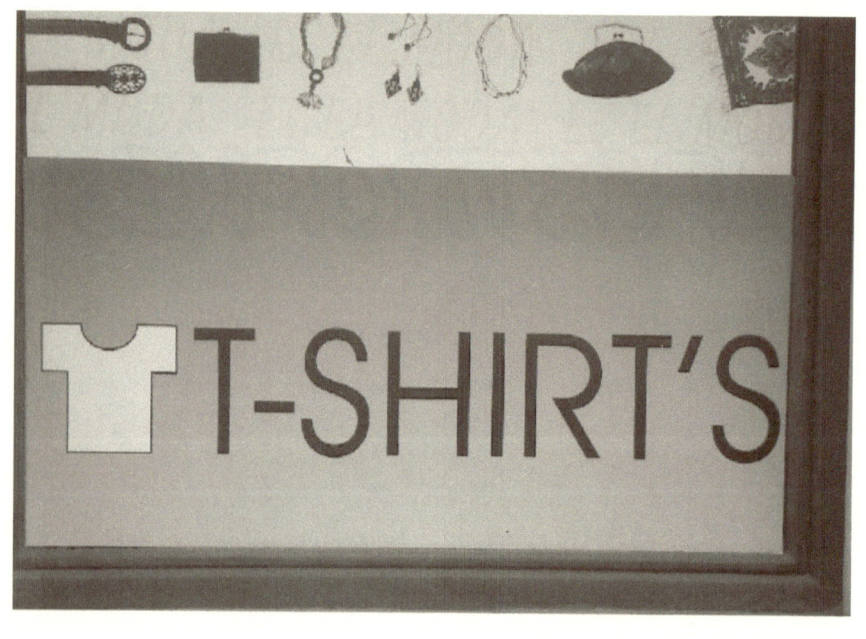

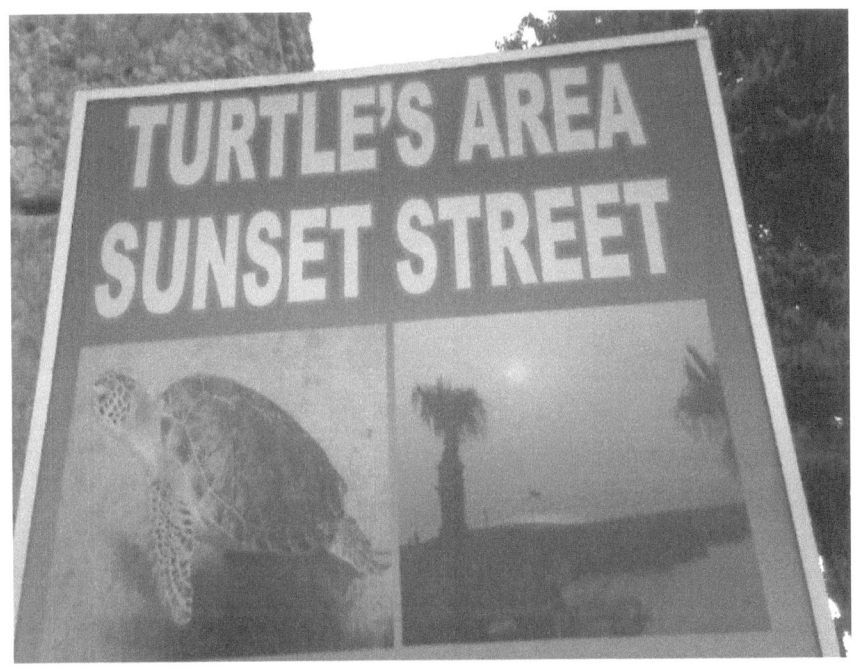

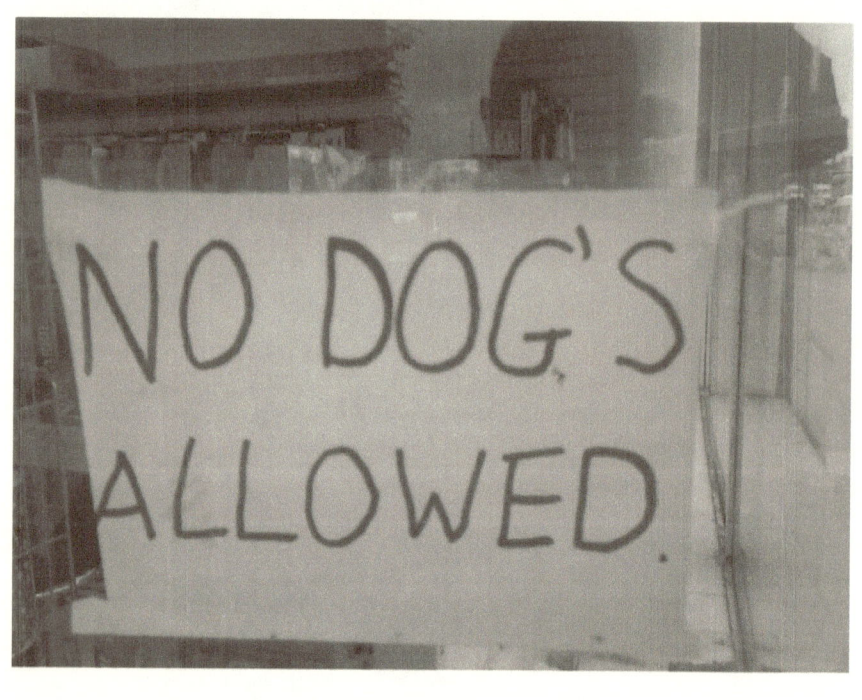

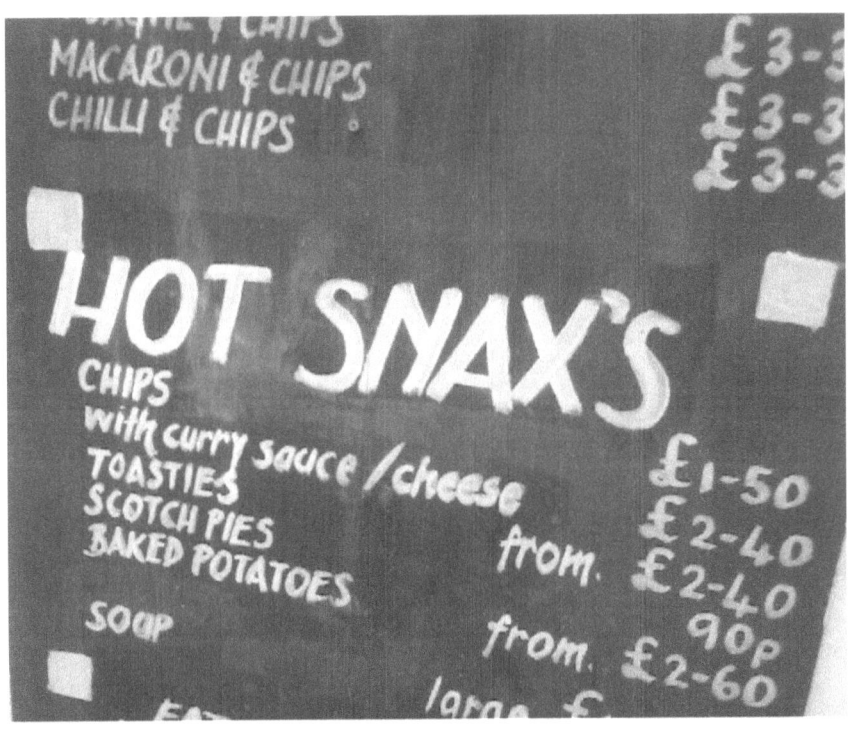

MACARONI & CHIPS   £3-3
CHILLI & CHIPS   £3-3
                     £3-3

HOT SNAX'S

CHIPS
with curry sauce /cheese   £1-50
TOASTIES
SCOTCH PIES   from.   £2-40
BAKED POTATOES   £2-40

soap   90p
                    from.   £2-60
                    large £

5

Urban Pind

INDIAN RESTAURANT

14 Candleriggs, Merchant City,
Glasgow, G1 1ED
www.urbanpind.co.uk · 0141-552 2812

Gift Voucher's Available

REPAIR BUMPER
RENEW GRILLE'S X2
DEFLECTOR.

£348 + VAT

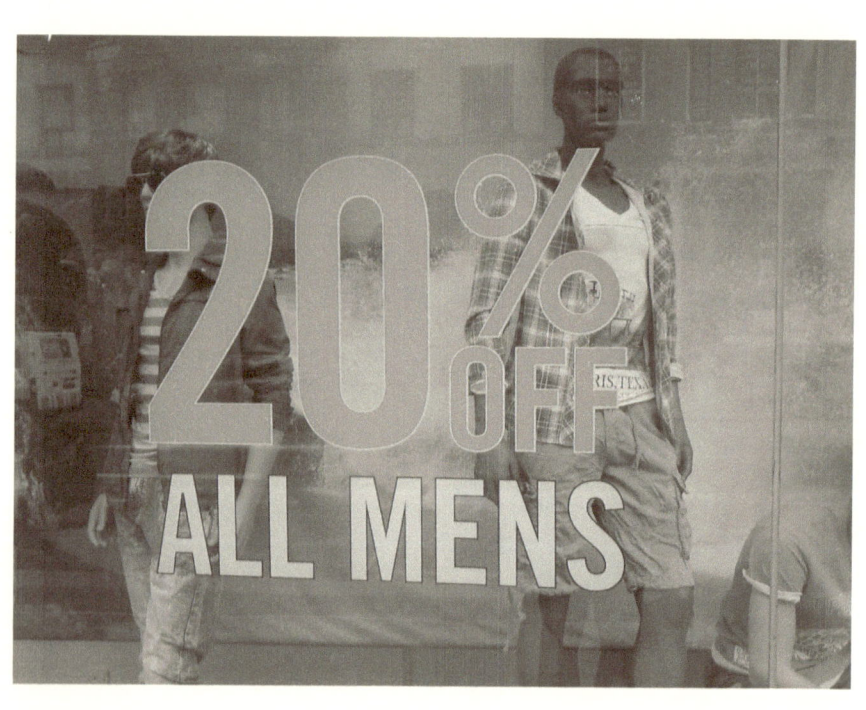

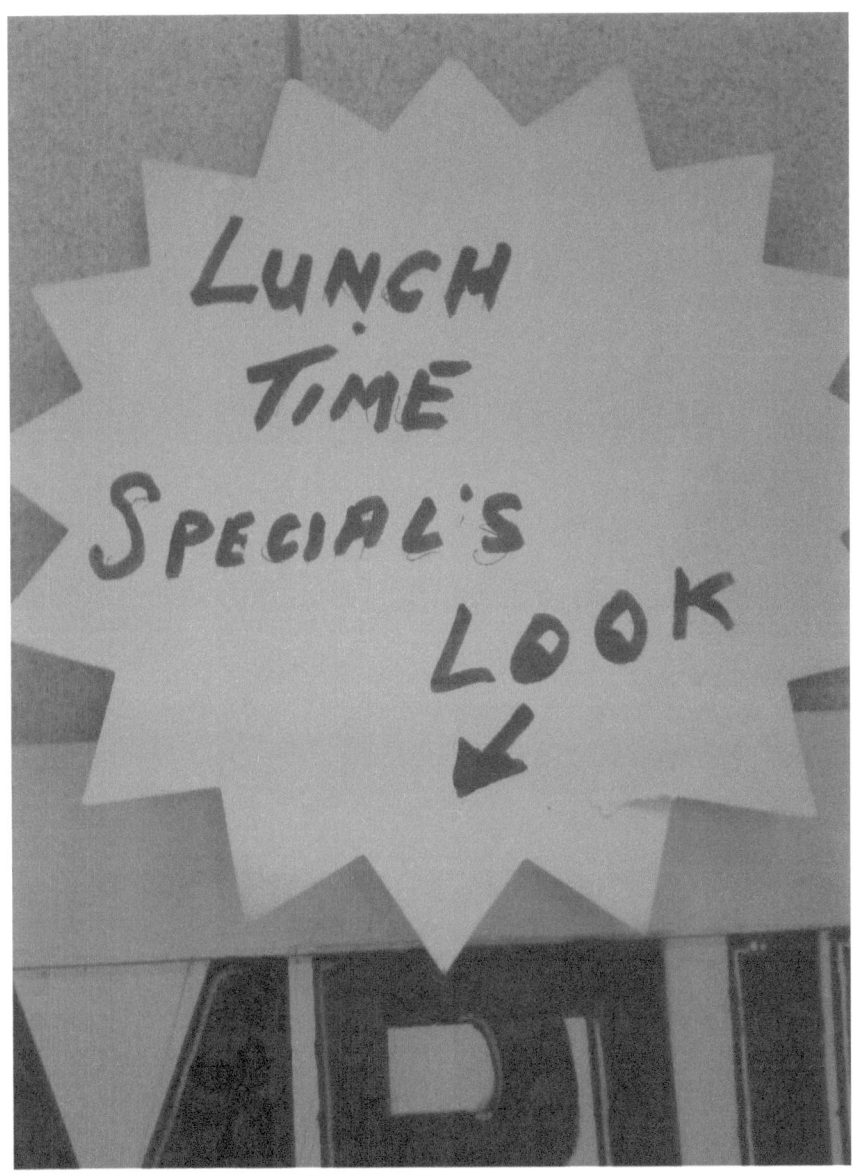

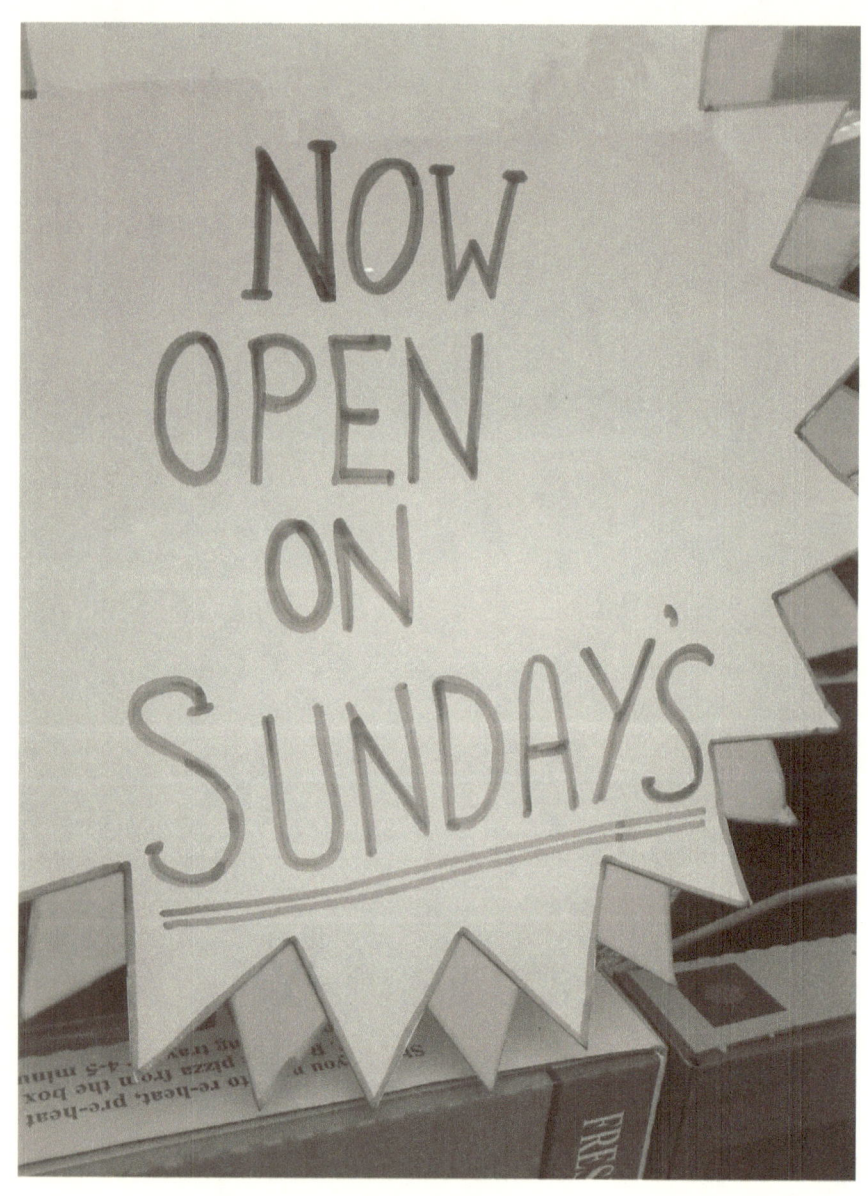

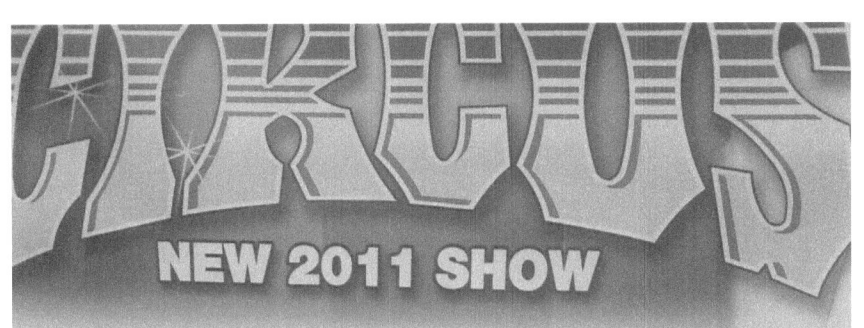

NEW 2011 SHOW

SCOTLAND'S FAVOURITE CIRCUS WILL VIS

CARDROSS

CIRCUS SITE, WESTERHILL FARM, CARDROSS ROAD G82 5E

SAT 9 JULY

PERFORMANCE TIMES:				
SAT 9th	SUN 10th	MON 11th	TUE 12th	WED 13th
2.30pm & 5pm	2.30pm & 5pm	2.30pm & 7.30pm	2.30pm & 7.30pm	2.30pm Only

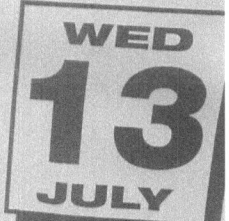

WED 13 JULY

Traditional Circus At It's Very Best!

£5 OFF VOUCHERS AVAILABLE IN LOCAL SHOPS AND ONLINE

BOX OFFICE OPEN ON SITE FROM FRIDAY 8TH JULY 10AM - 8PM DAILY

PRICES ADULTS: GRANDSTAND £15.00 RINGSIDE £18.00 ROYAL BOX: £20.00
PRICES CHILD/OAP: GRANDSTAND £12.00 RINGSIDE £15.00 ROYAL BOX: £18.00

SEATS AVAILABLE 30 MINS PRIOR TO PERFORMANCE

NO REFUNDS

DIAL-A-SEAT: 07860 787 745

DISCOUNT INTERNET BOOKING: www.bobby-roberts.co.uk

SEATS ALSO AVAILABLE FROM THE CIRCUS ON THE DAY

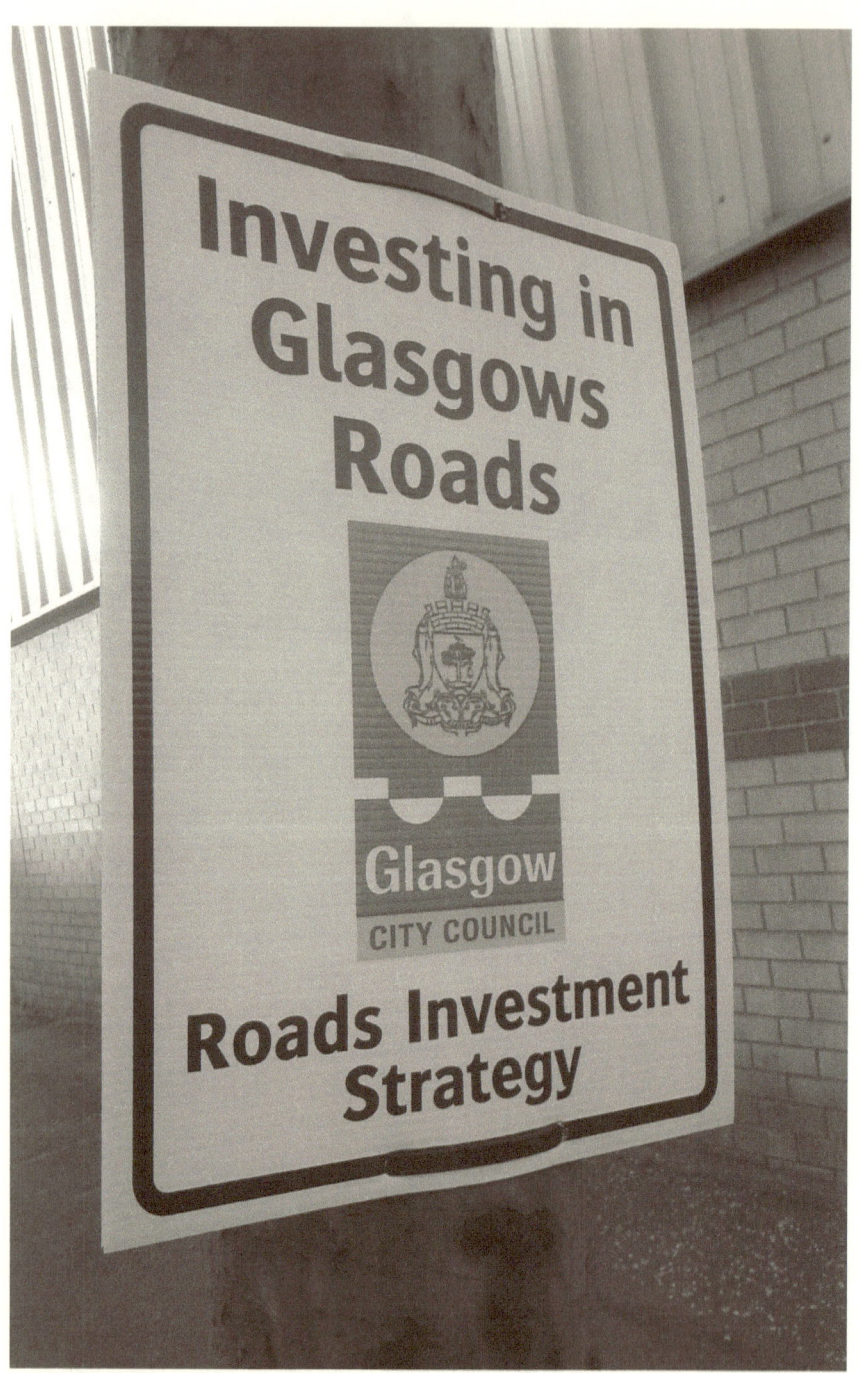

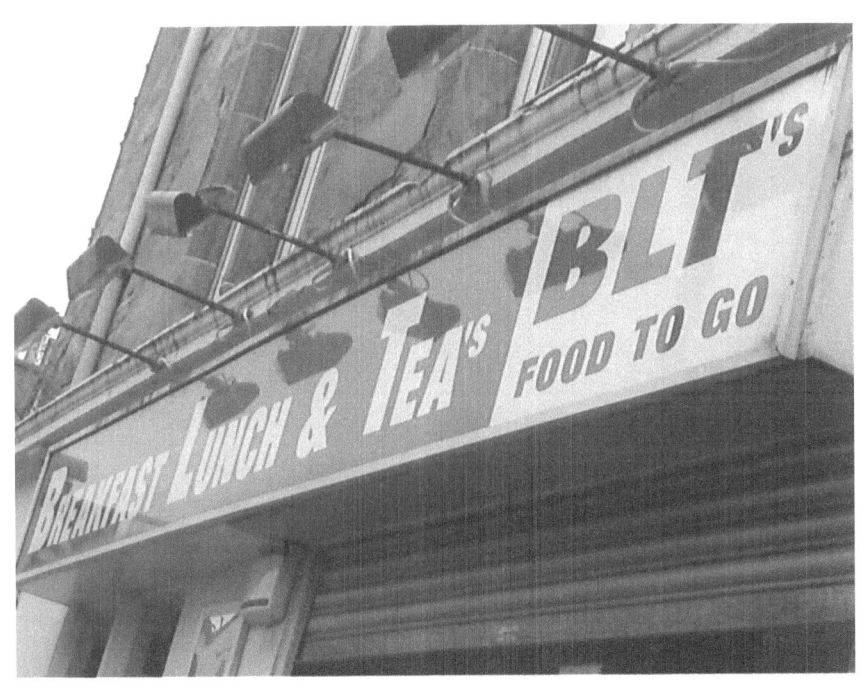

13

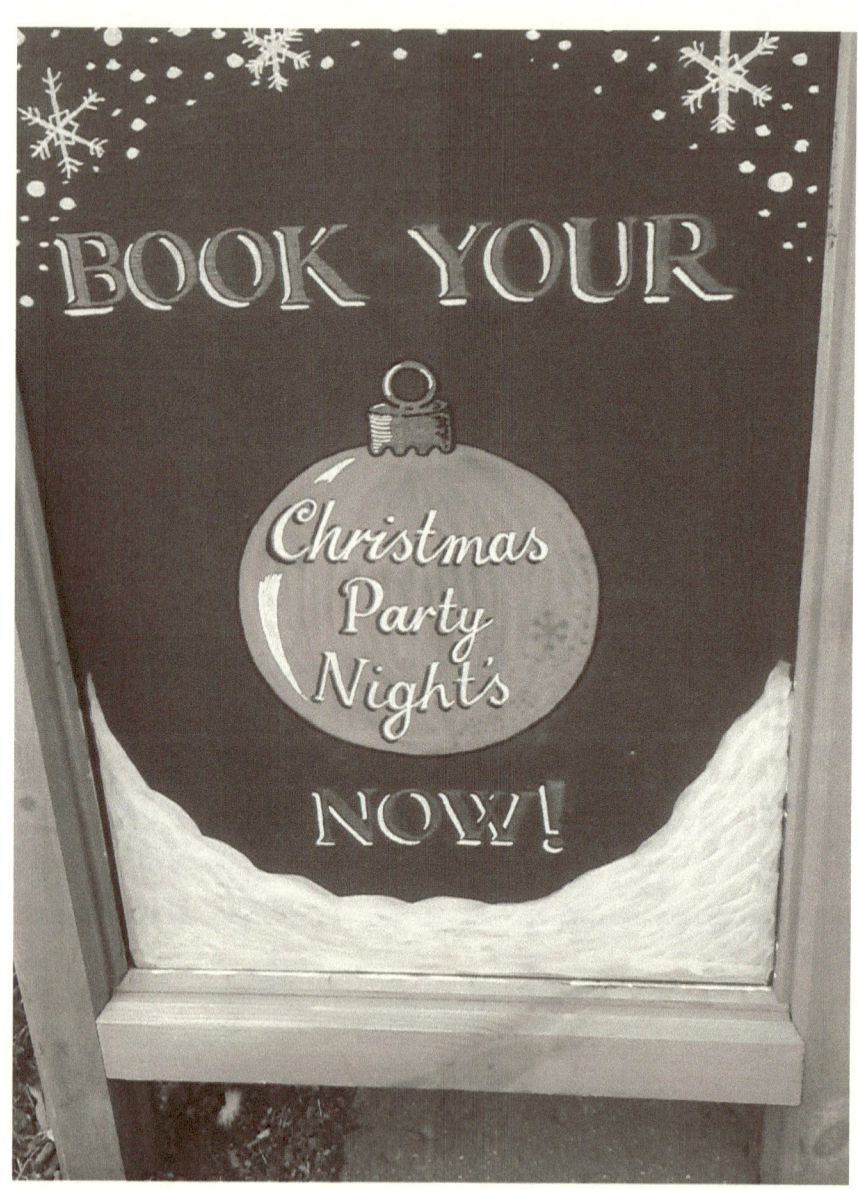

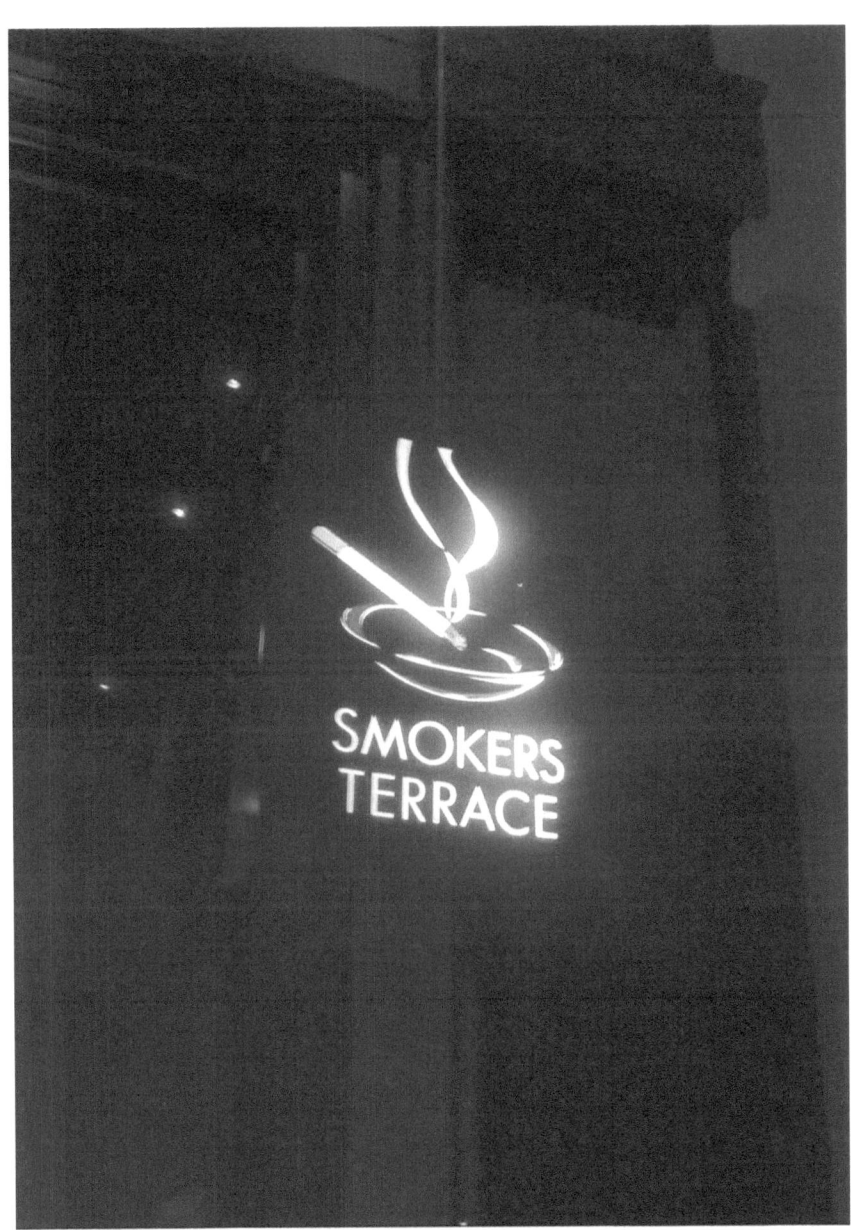

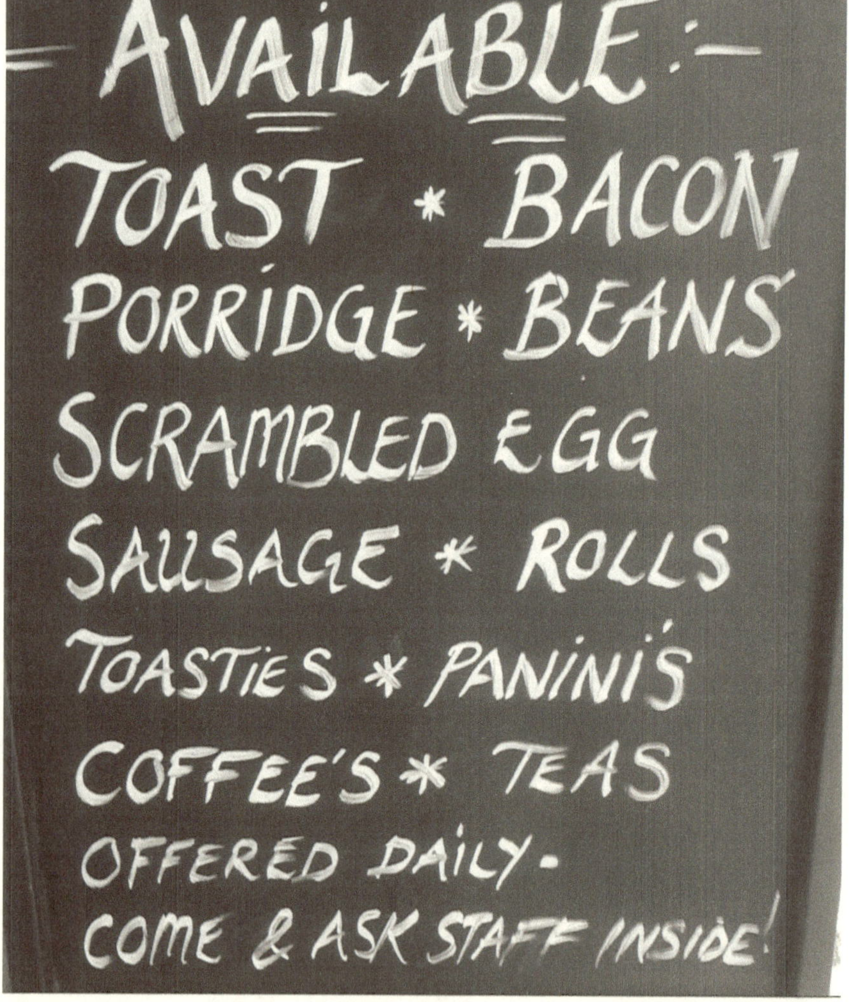

more inside

BREAKFAST

AVAILABLE:-

TOAST * BACON

PORRIDGE * BEANS

SCRAMBLED EGG

SAUSAGE * ROLLS

TOASTIES * PANINI'S

COFFEE'S * TEAS

OFFERED DAILY.

COME & ASK STAFF INSIDE!

Dessert's

Caramel apple pie.
Strawberry cheesecake.
mandarin Cheesecake.
hot cookie + icecream.
black forrest gateau.
Strawberry gateau.
Christmas pudding.

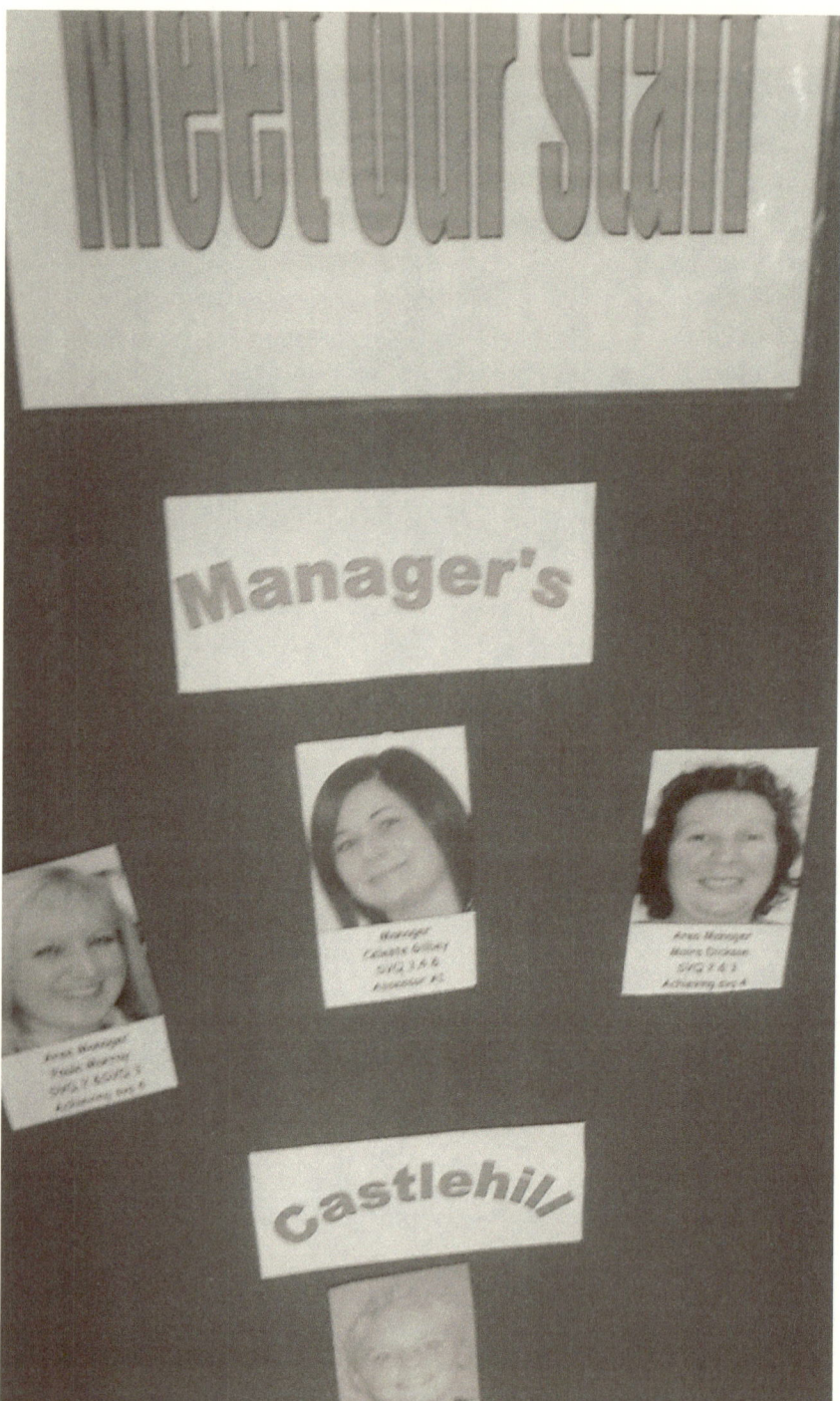

19

GEORGE MEWES
CHEESE

CHEESE
OF THE MONTH
STICHELTON

Made by Joe Sneider·
at Welbeck Estate
Nottinghamshire.
—
Its an unpasteurised
Organic Cows Milk
Blue Cheese.
—
Please come in
for a wee taste

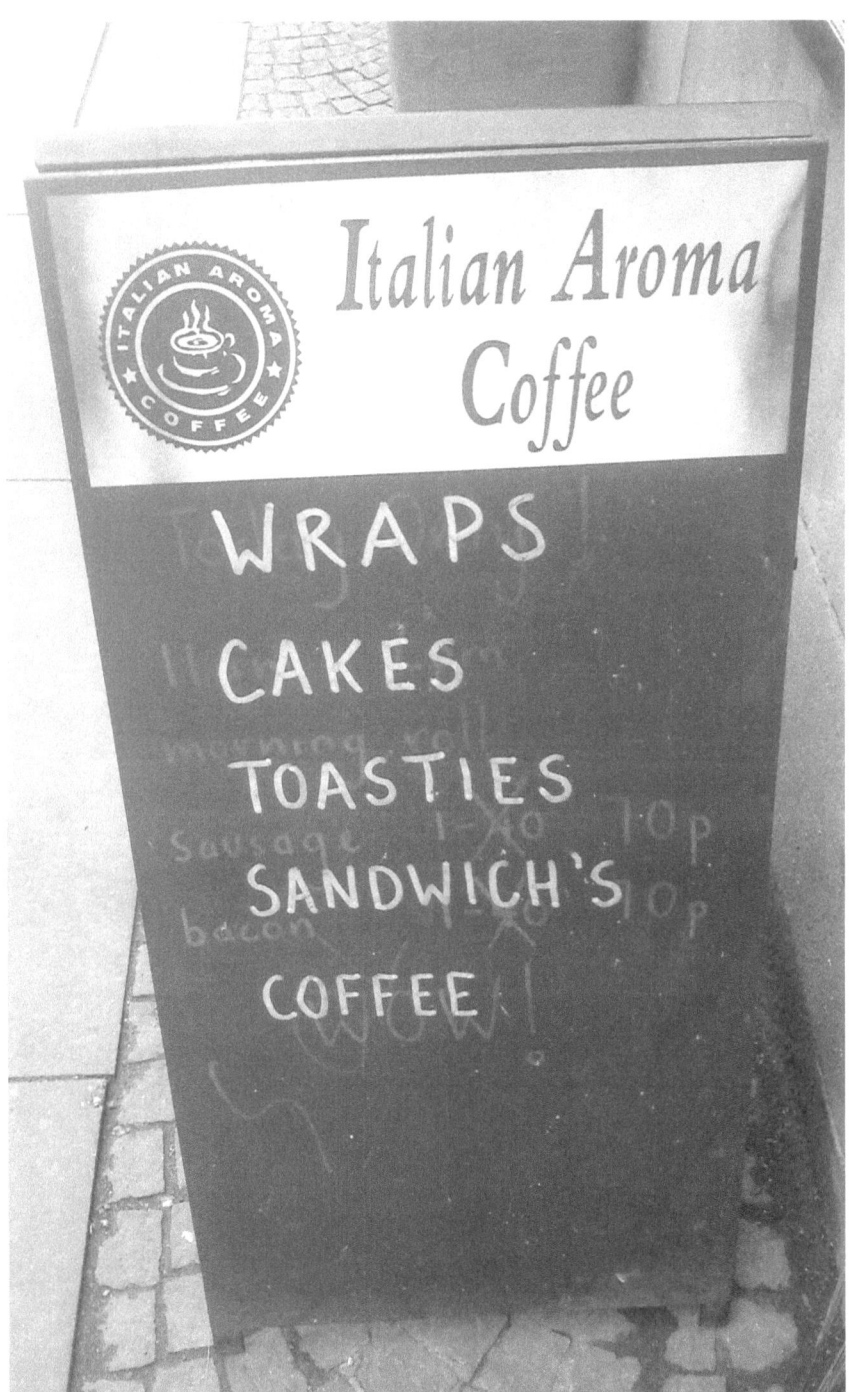

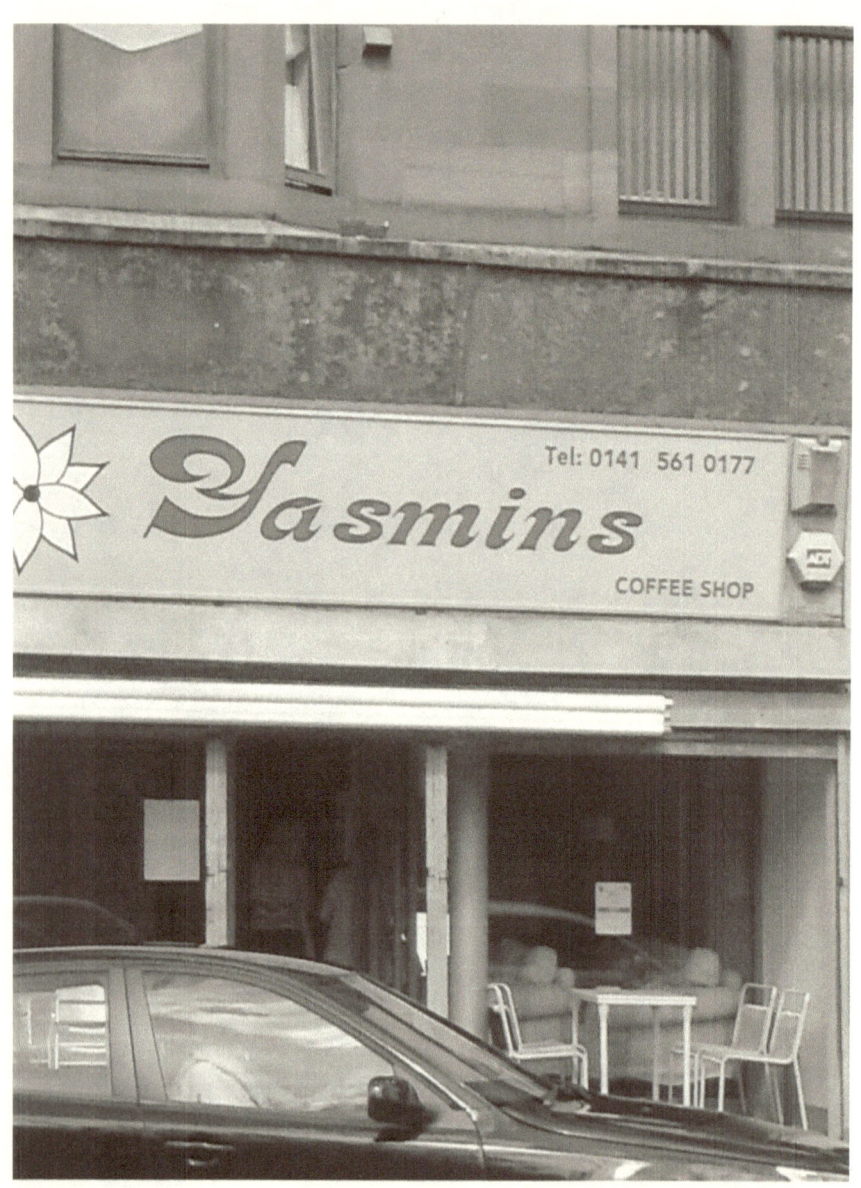

SALADS

£4.95

Chicken Caesar Salad
Chicken Breast and Bacon, Crisp Lettuce, Croutons and Parmesan
all covered in a Creamy Caesar Dressing.

Honey Roast Ham and Pineapple Salad
Slices of Honey Roast Ham topped with Pineapple and
served with Coleslaw   £4.95

Tuna Mayo
Tuna Mayo with Spring Onion, Lettuce, Tomatoes,
Cucumber all smothered in a Creamy Dressing   £4.95

Prawn Salad
Fresh Prawns served with a Marie Rose Mayo on a bed of
Crisp Lettuce and topped with a Zesty Slice of Lemon   £4.95

ALL DAY BREAKFAST

Bacon, Sausage, Black Pudding, Potato Scone, Fried Egg,
Beans and Tomato served with Buttered Toast.   £4.95

Plate of Chips	£1.70
Beans on Toast	£2.30
Scrambled Egg on Toast	£2.00

MAIN COURSES

Fish 'n Chips	£5.95
Scampi 'n Chips	£5.95
Chicken Goujons with Chips	£3.95

SPECIALITY TEA'S AND COFFEE'S AVAILABLE FROM £1.50

SELECT A CAKE FROM OUR TEMPTING CABINET FROM £1.00

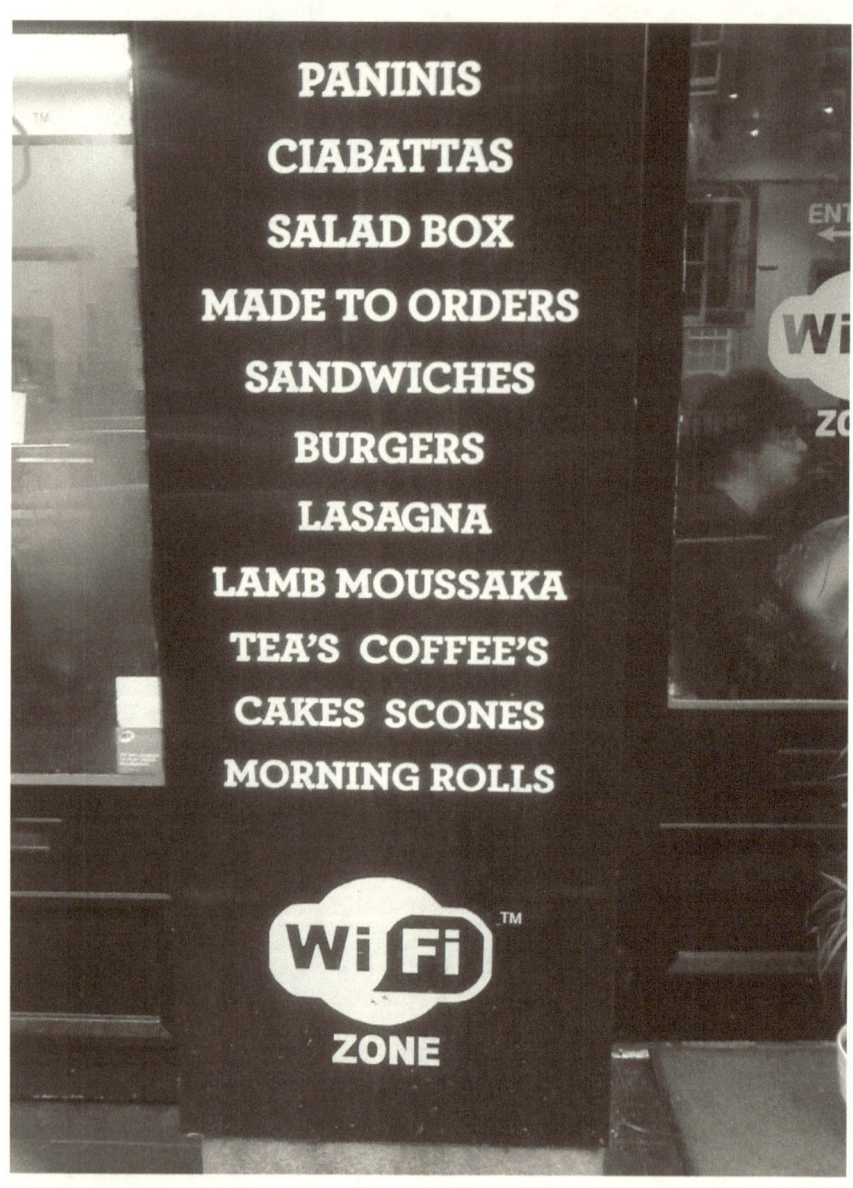

PANINIS
CIABATTAS
SALAD BOX
MADE TO ORDERS
SANDWICHES
BURGERS
LASAGNA
LAMB MOUSSAKA
TEA'S COFFEE'S
CAKES SCONES
MORNING ROLLS

Wi Fi™
ZONE

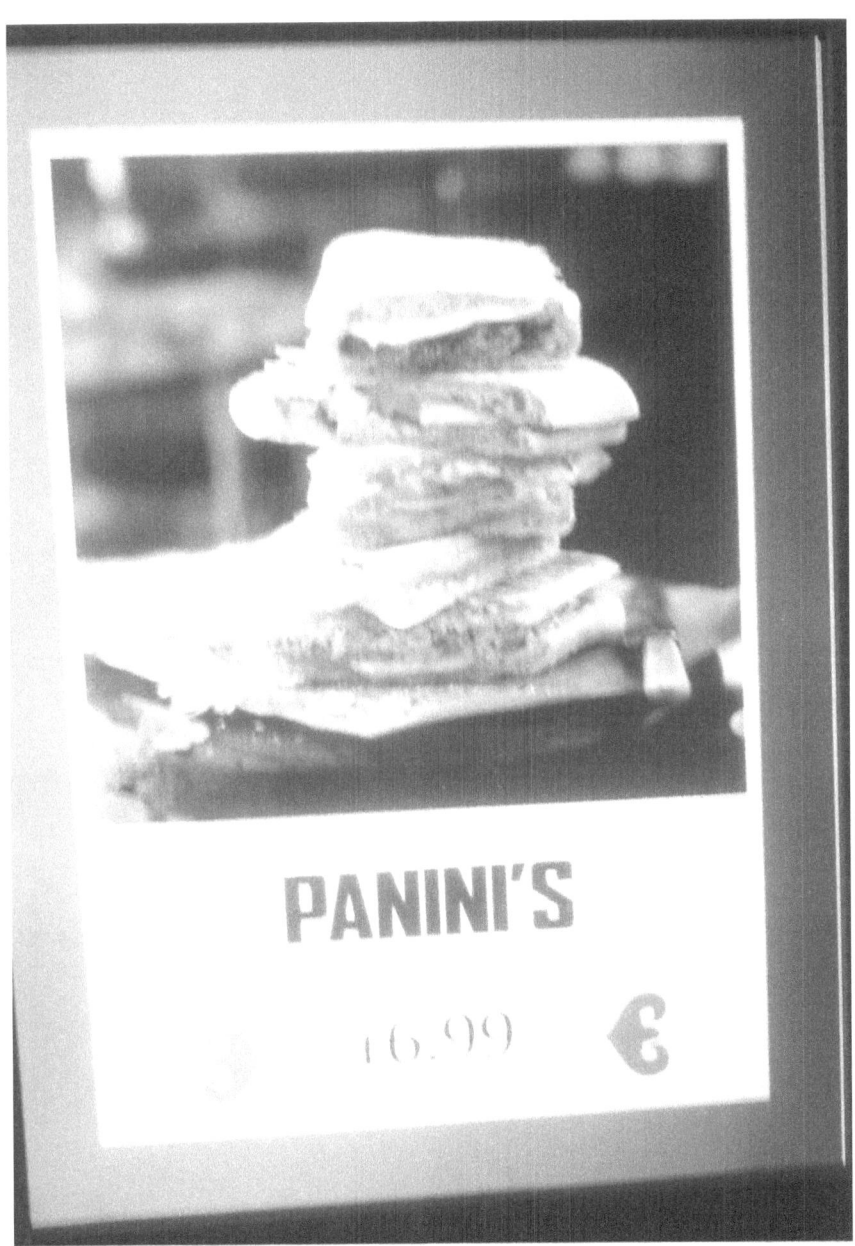

PANINI'S

€6.99

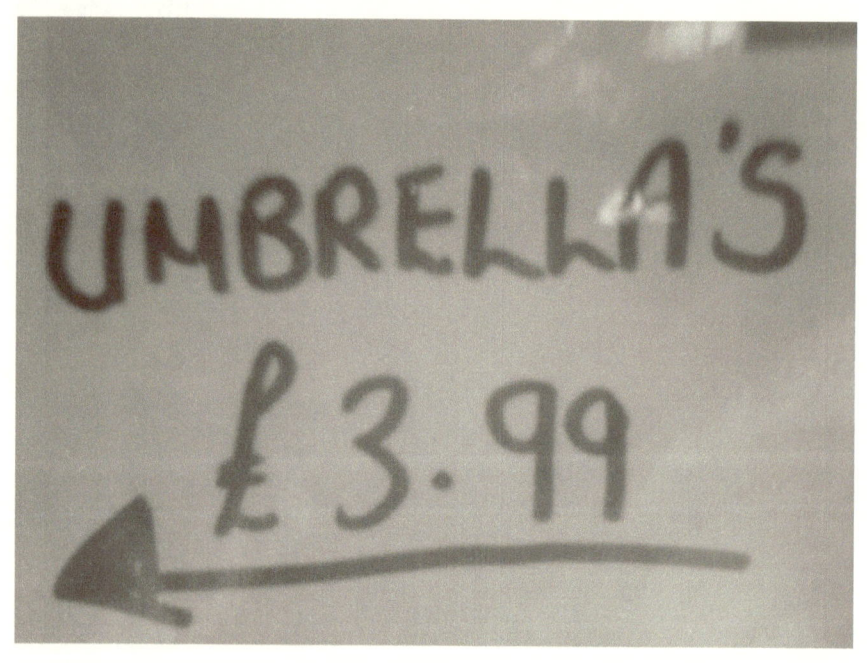

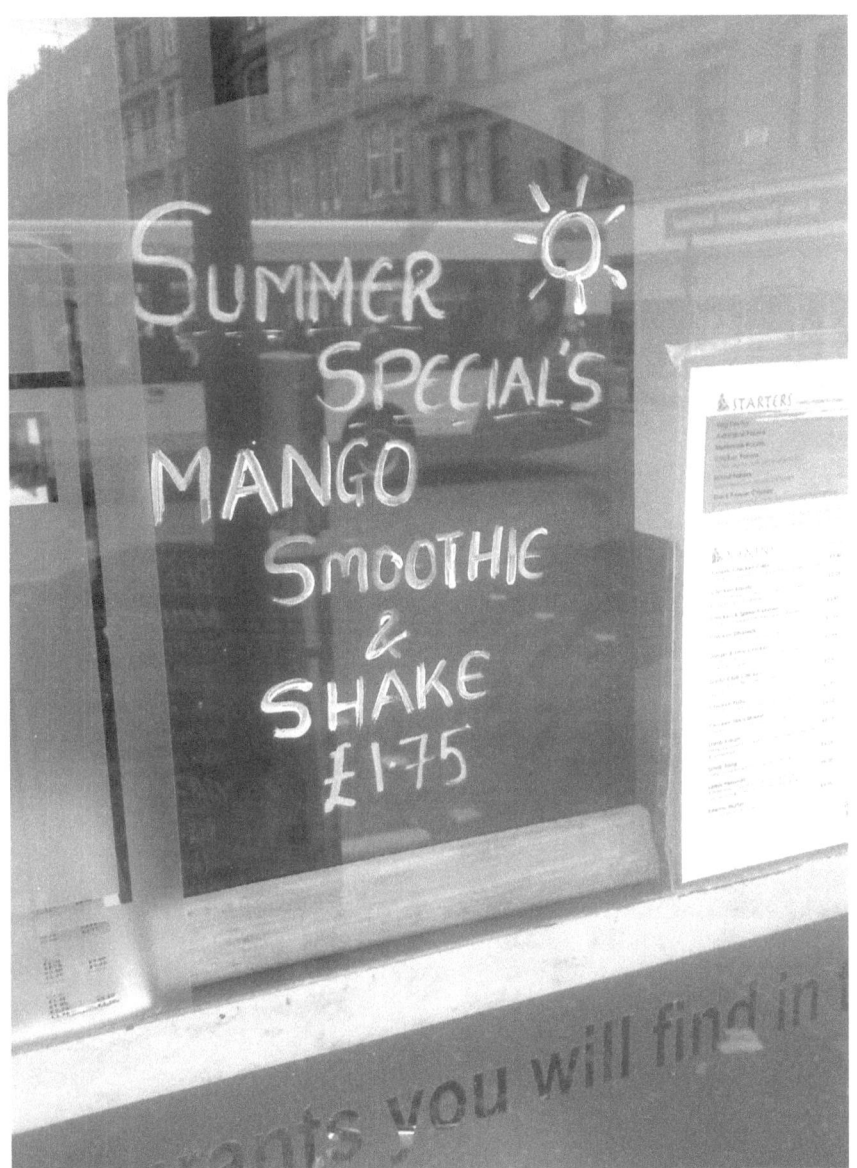

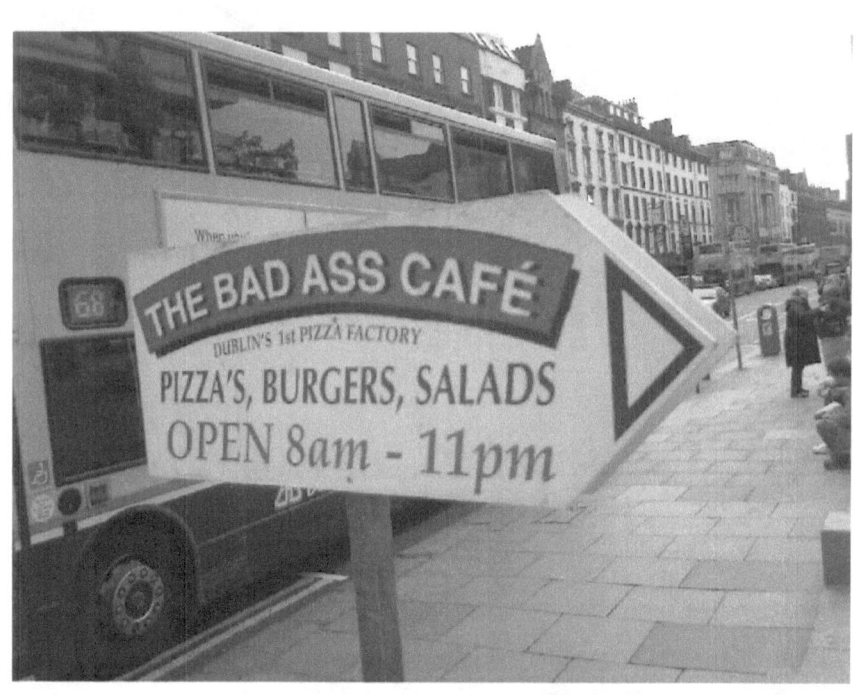

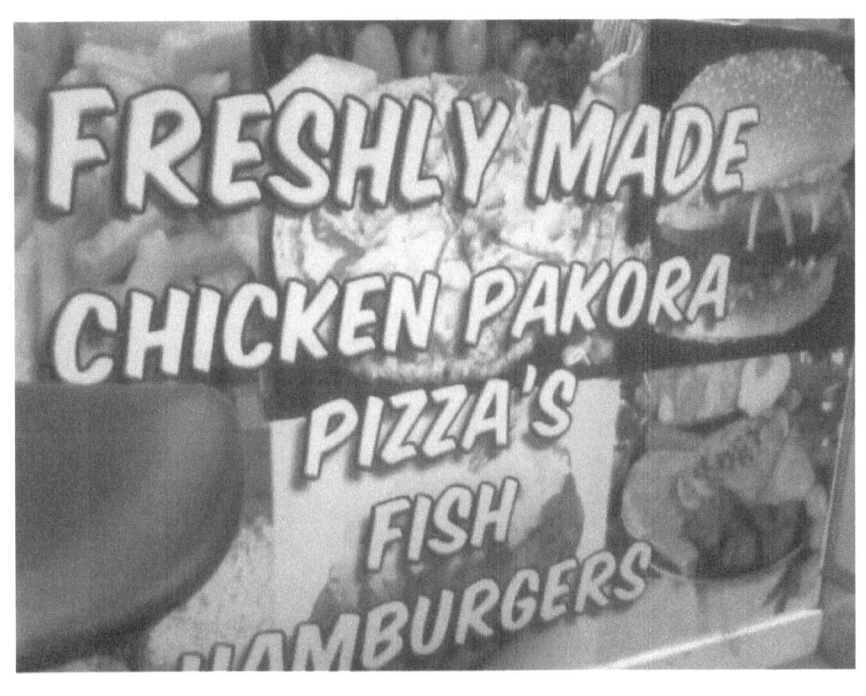

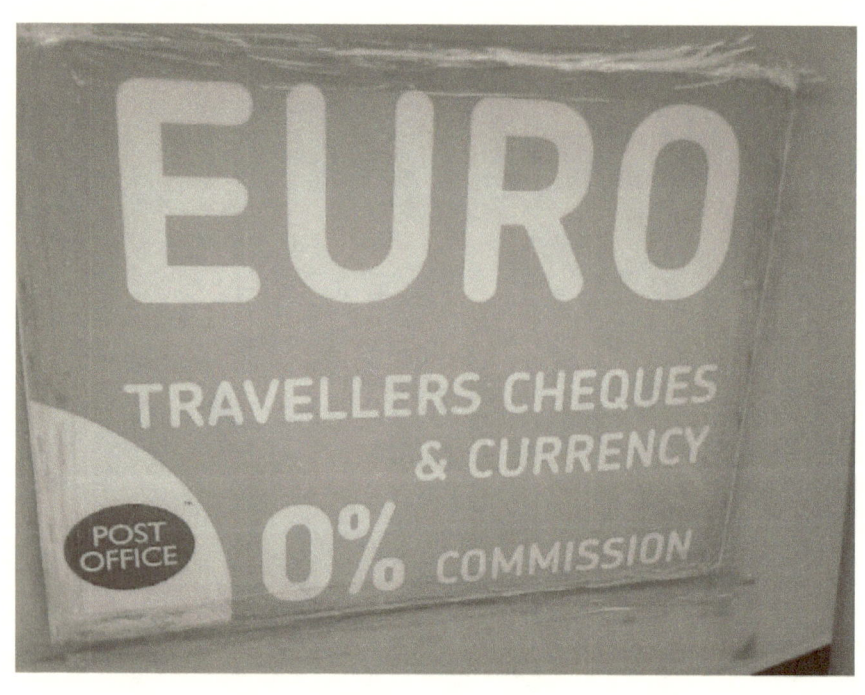

Inflatable's – £2 each
All money raised will go towards
Ronald McDonalds House Charity.
Please ask any member of staff.

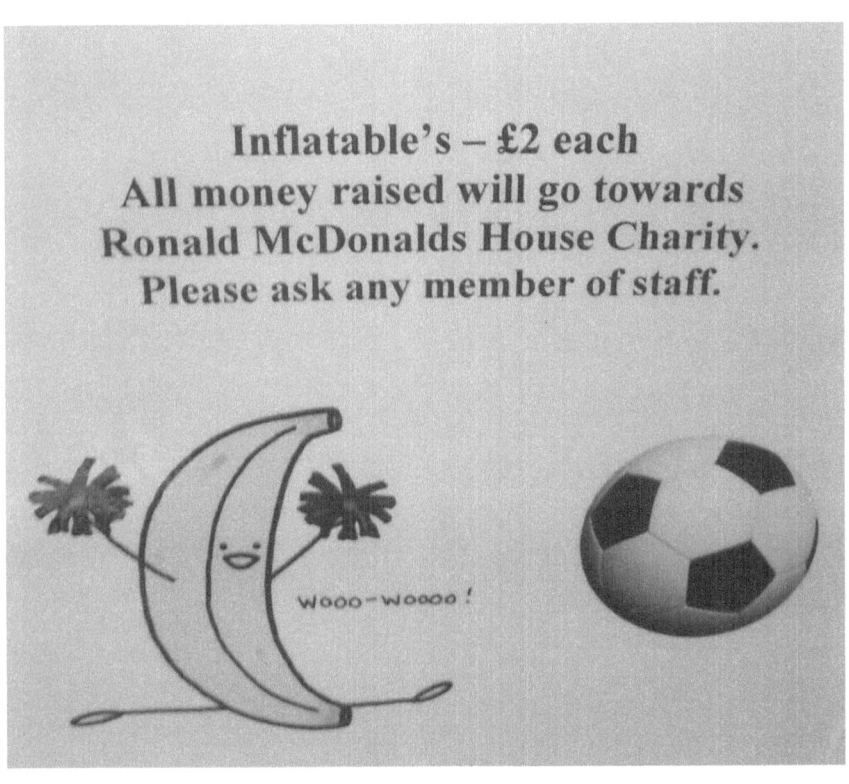

APOSTROPHES AND SPELLING!

censed CAFe is opeNed
untill 10 PM MON - SAt 6 PM SU
ow serving
Hot SPeCIALS from 5 PM untill 9 PM.

tonight's Special is...

Beef and ale stew with a
puff pastry parcel

£9.95

And for something sweet
try and todays desserts...

tonight's
Staff
favourite

Brioche bread and butter
pudding
with pouring cream

34

COFFEE MORNINGS

A CHANCE TO MEET NEW MUMS FROM YOUR LOCAL AREA TO SWAP ADVICE ON SLEEPLESS NIGHTS OR JUST FOR A GENERAL CHIT CHAT.

WE ALL KNOW YOU EAT, SLEEP TALK BABIES NOW IS THE CHANCE TO HAVE A CONVERSATION WITH OTHER MUMS.

WE AT MCDONALDS MILNGAVIE ARE INVITING MUMS AND BABIES/TODDLERS TO JOIN US AT OUR COFFEE MORNINGS.

EVERY TUESDAY MORNING AT 10 AM WERE WE WILL OFFER A BACON ROLL AND A COFFEE FOR £1.99

HOPE TO SEE TOU ALL THERE !!!

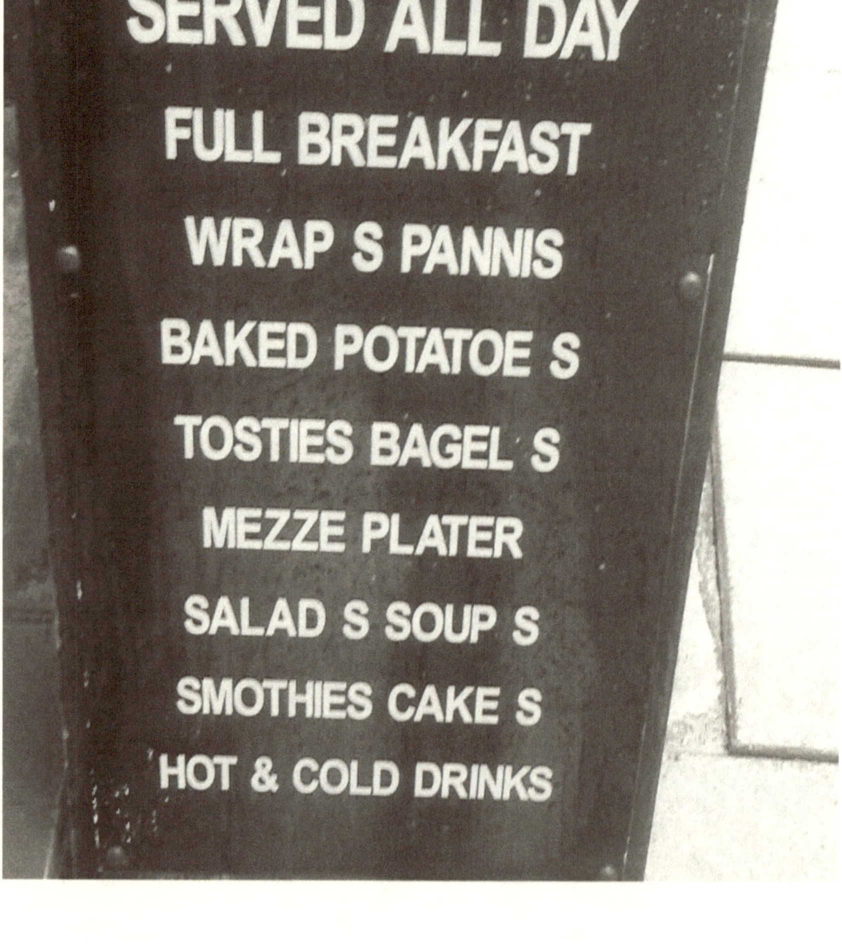

◀ café

SERVED ALL DAY

FULL BREAKFAST

WRAP S PANNIS

BAKED POTATOE S

TOSTIES BAGEL S

MEZZE PLATER

SALAD S SOUP S

SMOTHIES CAKE S

HOT & COLD DRINKS

al Tanner

program has been started ,

ically turned on at maximum setting (II).

press the "+" button. If you press the "-"

he facial tanners will be switched off completly.

u can re-activate the facial tanners or increase

al tanners have been switched off you can can

of 3 minutes. If you want to re-activate them

n to have your request registered and the facial

utomatically as soon as the 3 minutes are over.

ial tanners in the coin-operated system, you can

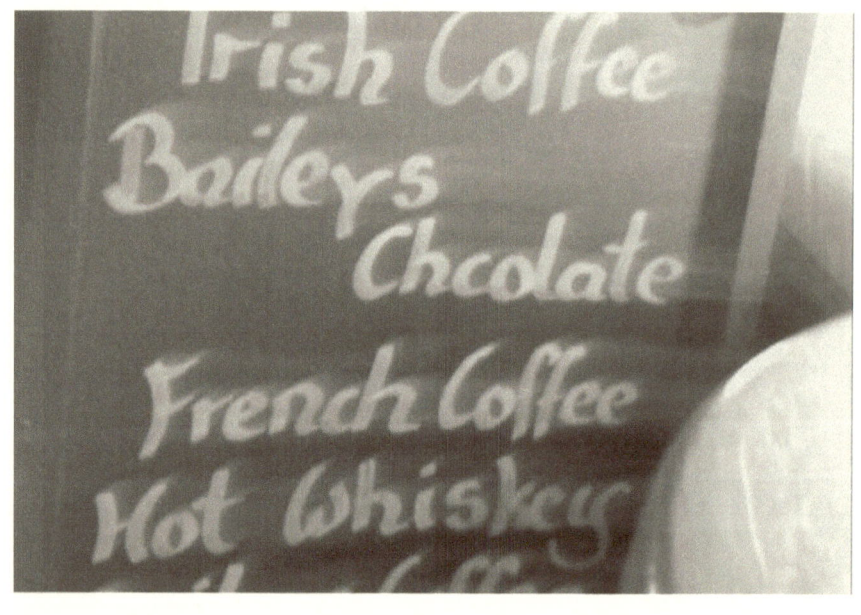

ONE WRONG, ONE RIGHT!

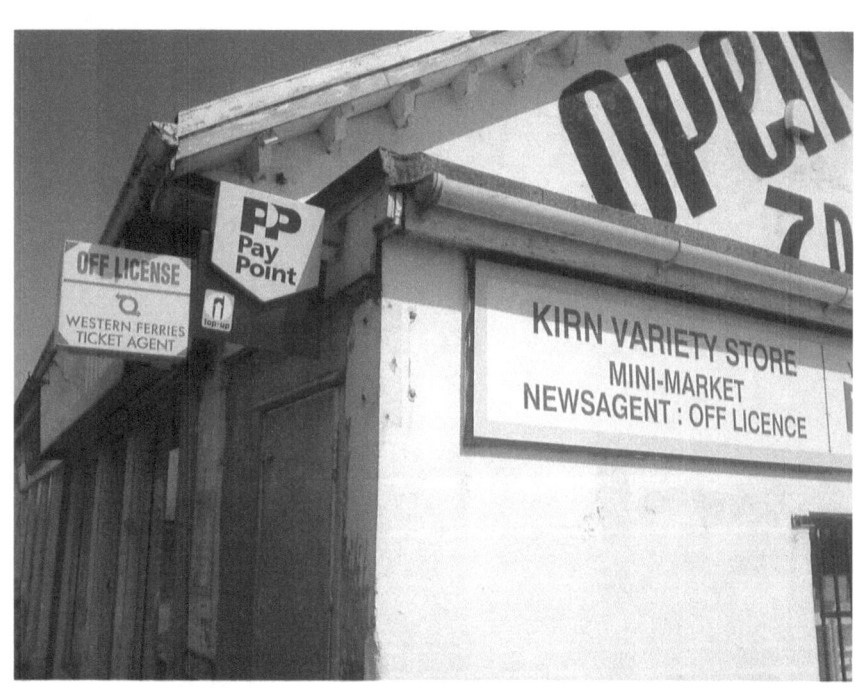

40

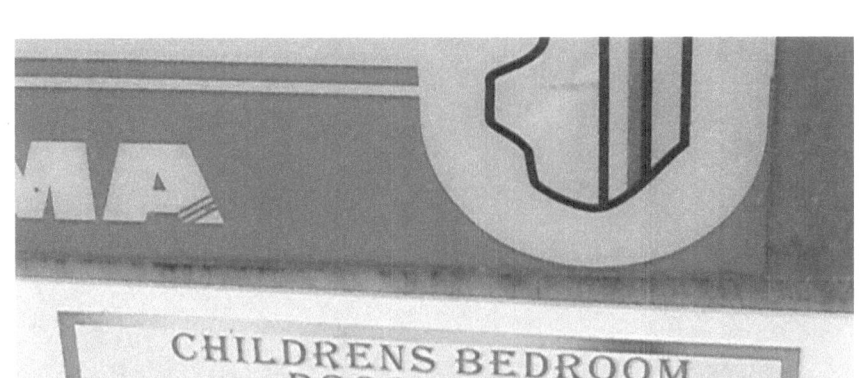

CHILDRENS BEDROOM DOOR SIGNS

CAN BE MADE TO ANY SIZE AT AN EXTRA COST

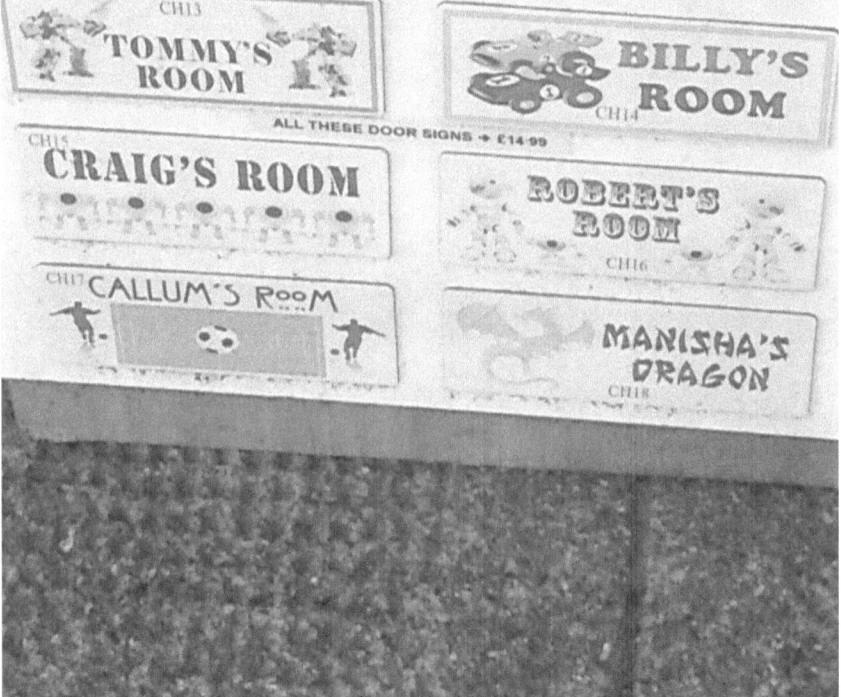

CH13 TOMMY'S ROOM

BILLY'S ROOM CH14

ALL THESE DOOR SIGNS → £14·99

CH15 CRAIG'S ROOM

ROBERT'S ROOM CH16

CH17 CALLUM'S ROOM

MANISHA'S DRAGON CH18

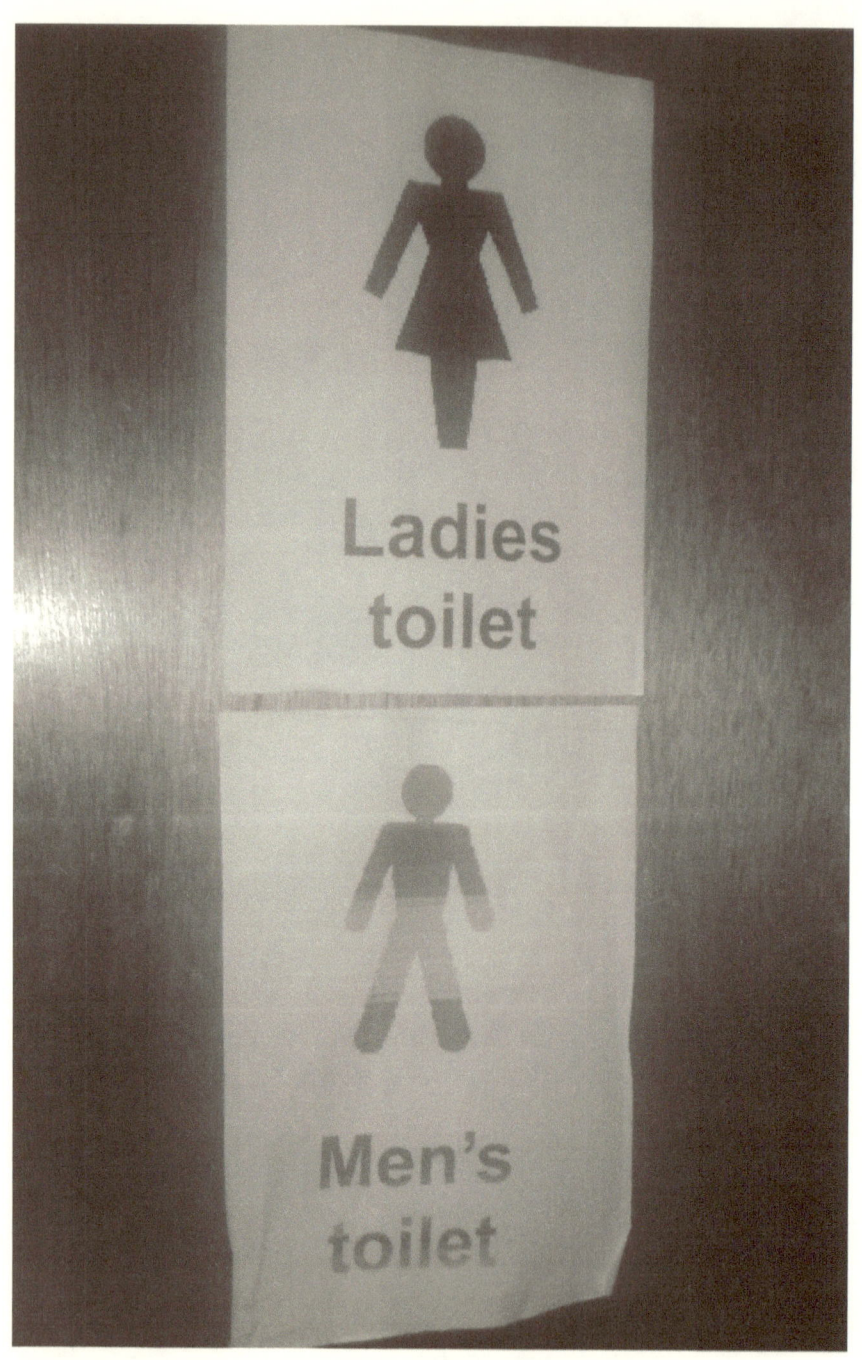

You're the pilot of an airplane that travels from New York to Chicago - a distance of 800 miles. The airplane travels at 200 mph and makes one stop for 30 minutes. What's the pilots name?

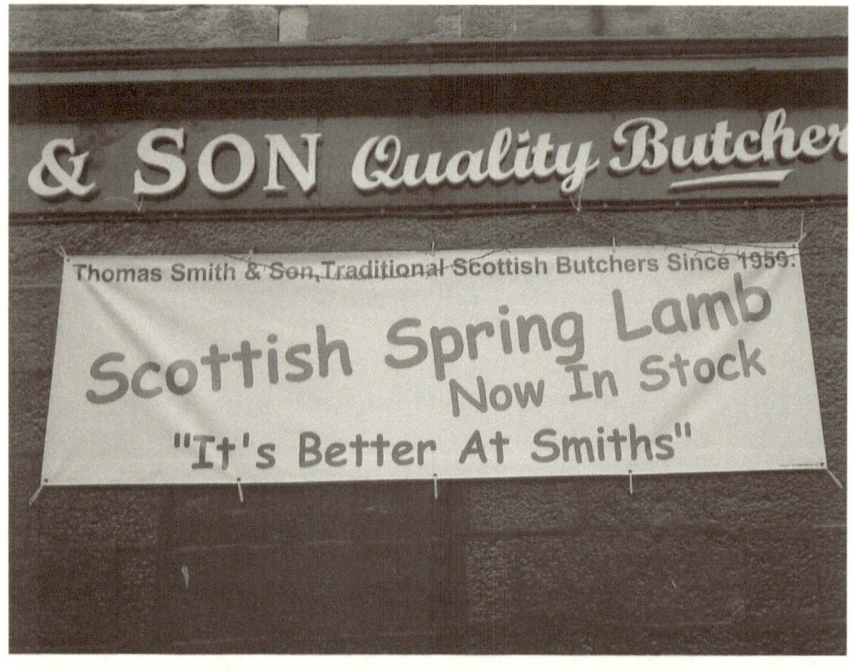

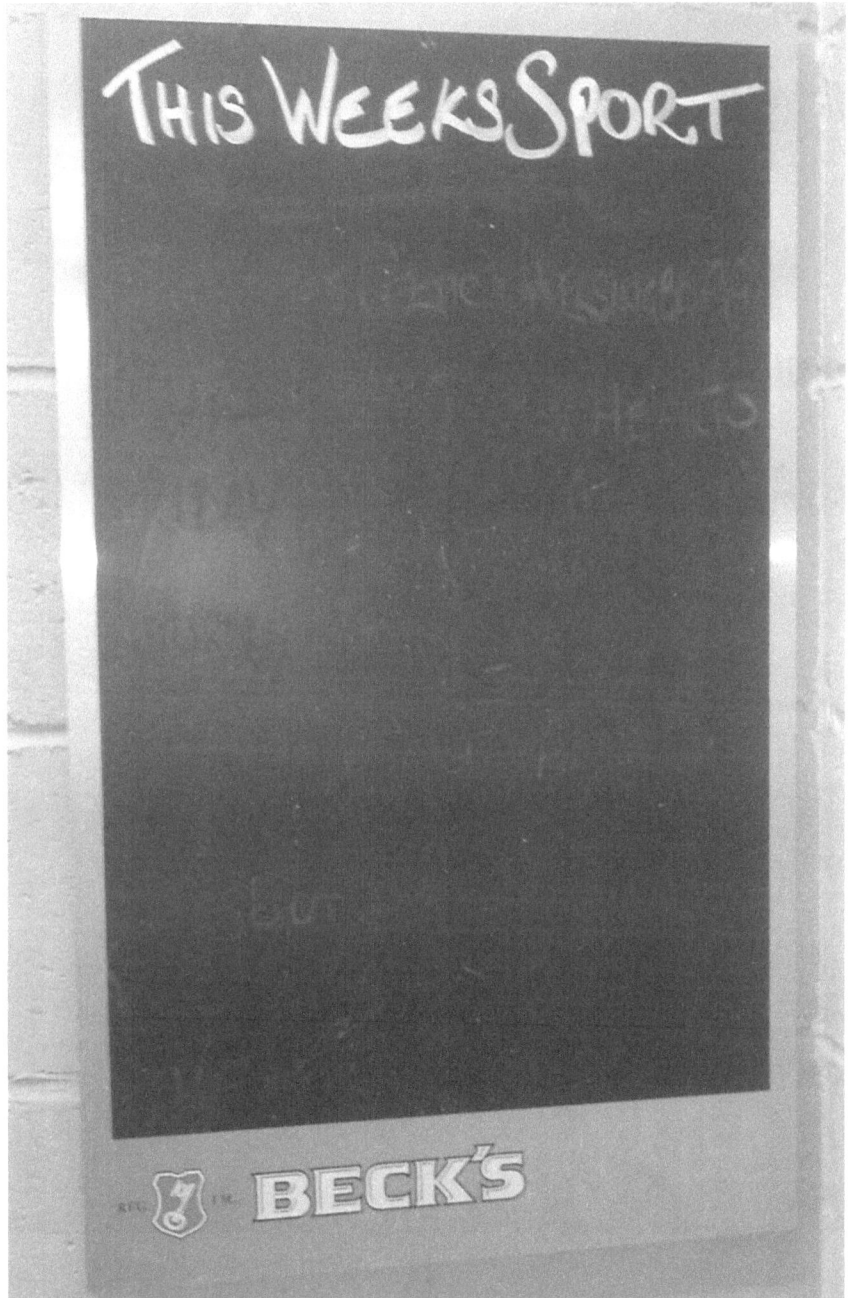

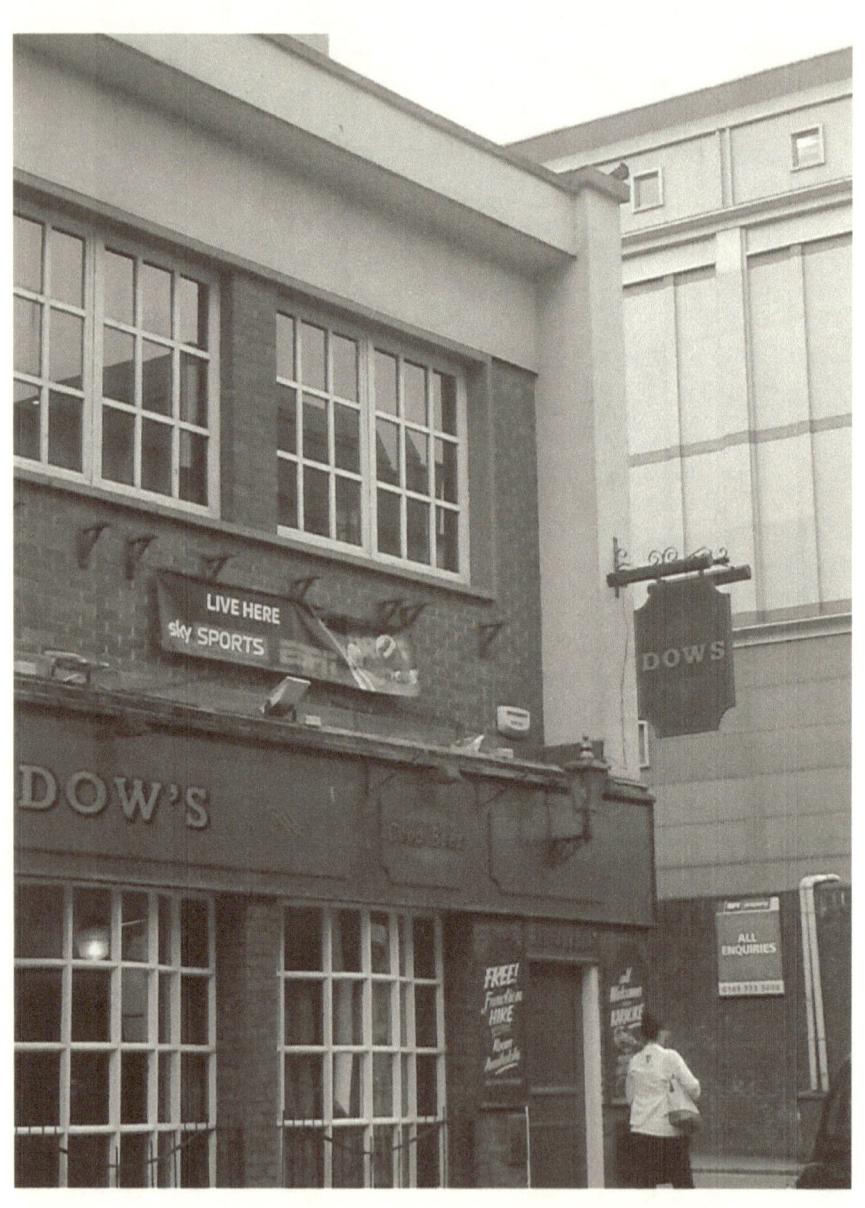

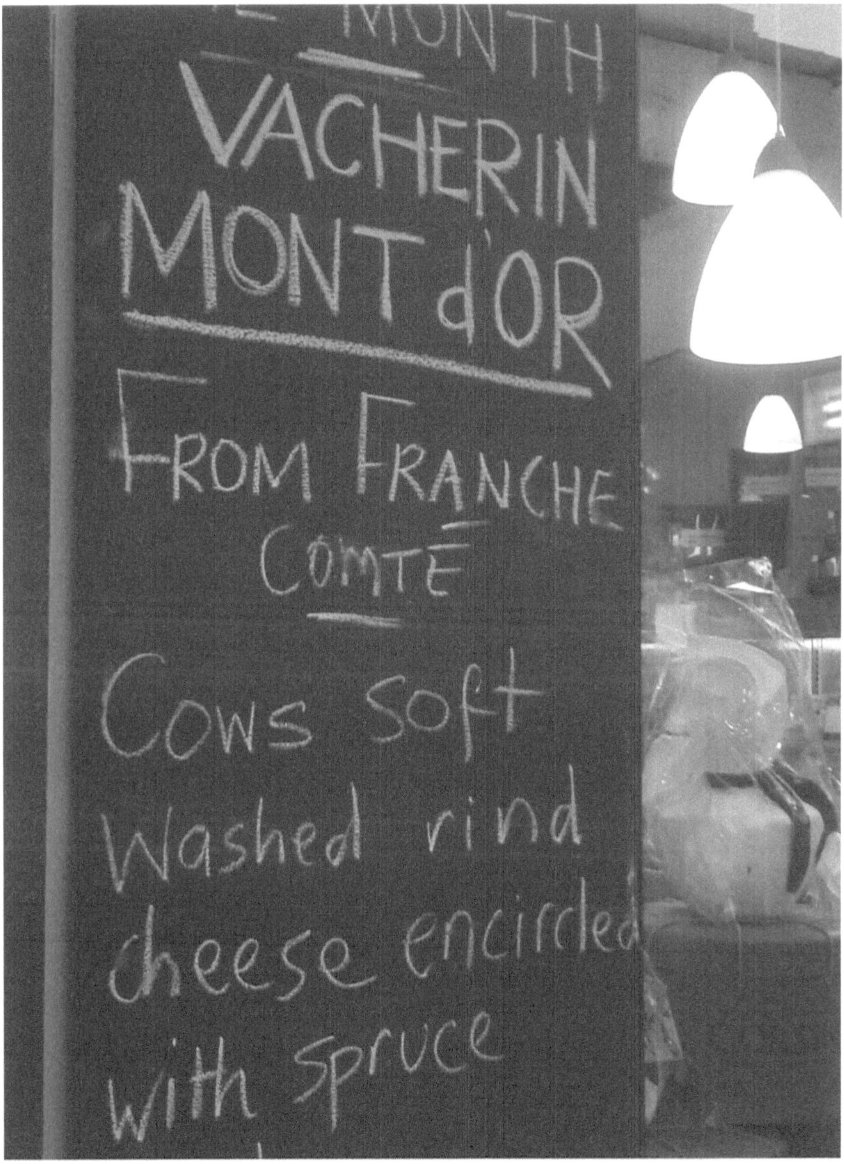

VACHERIN
MONT d'OR

FROM FRANCHE
COMTÉ

Cows soft
Washed rind
cheese encircled
with spruce

47

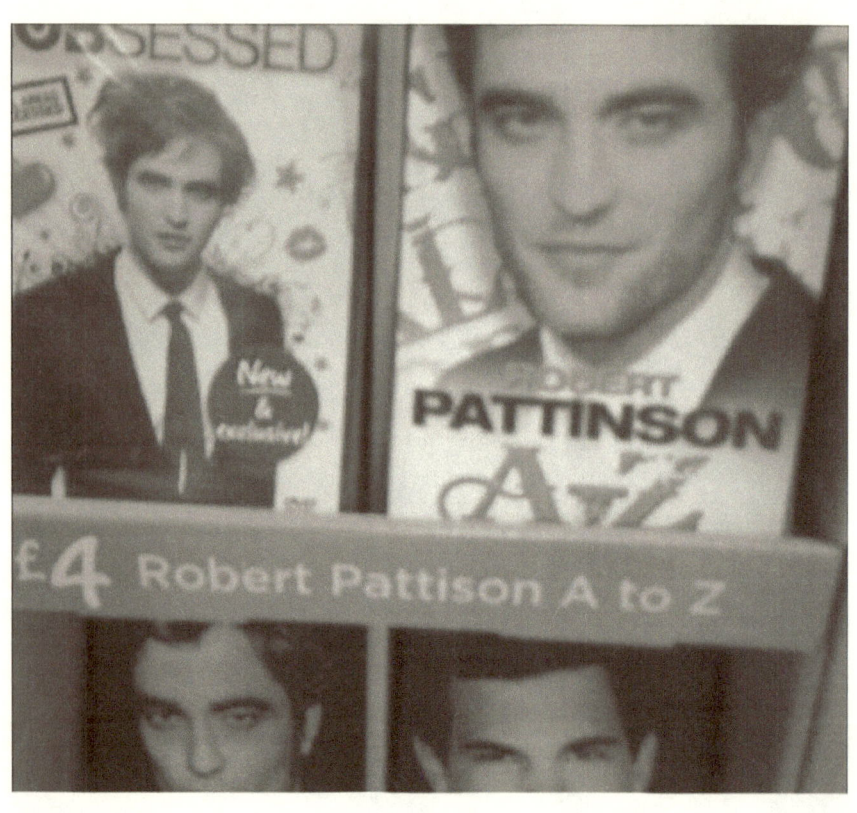

48

SPELLING

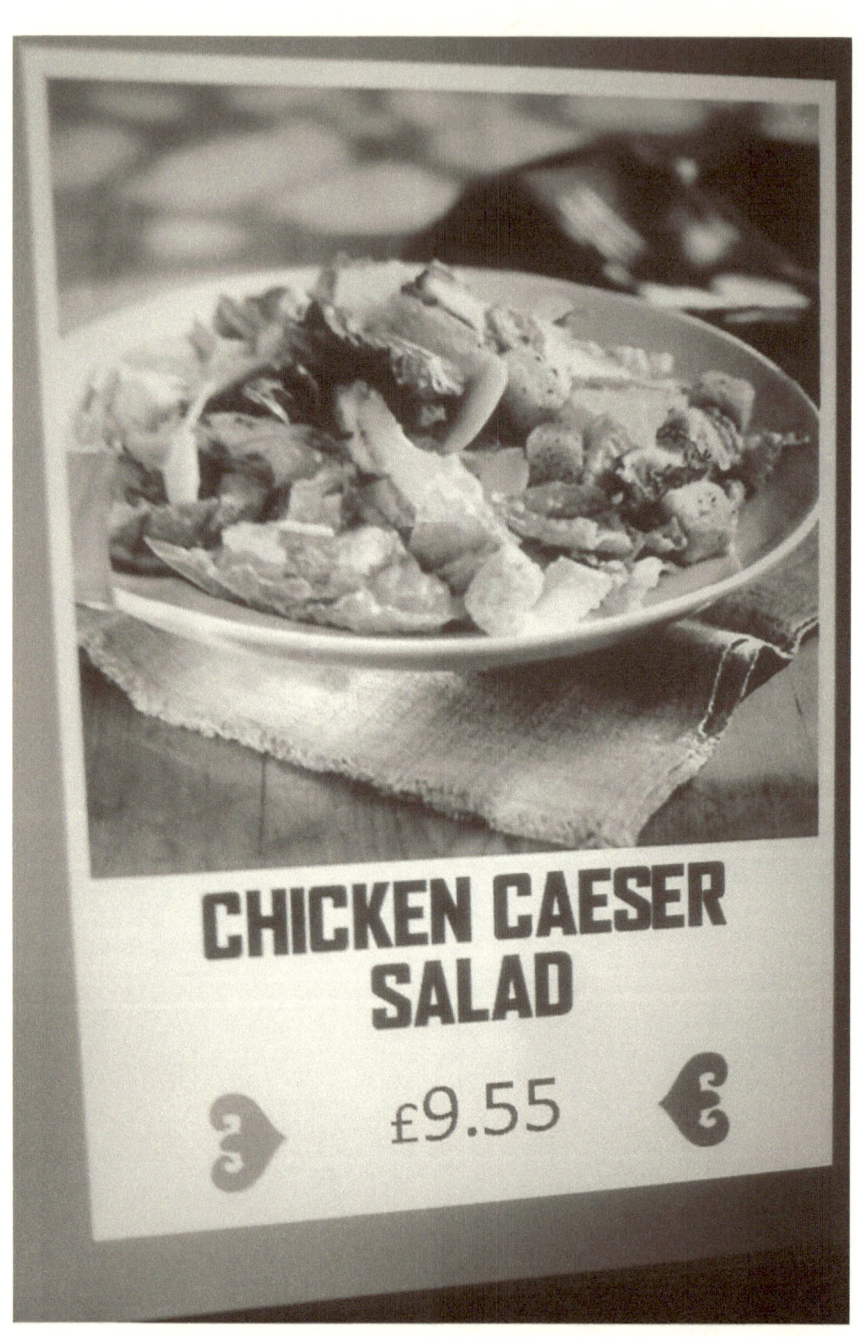

CHICKEN CAESER SALAD

£9.55

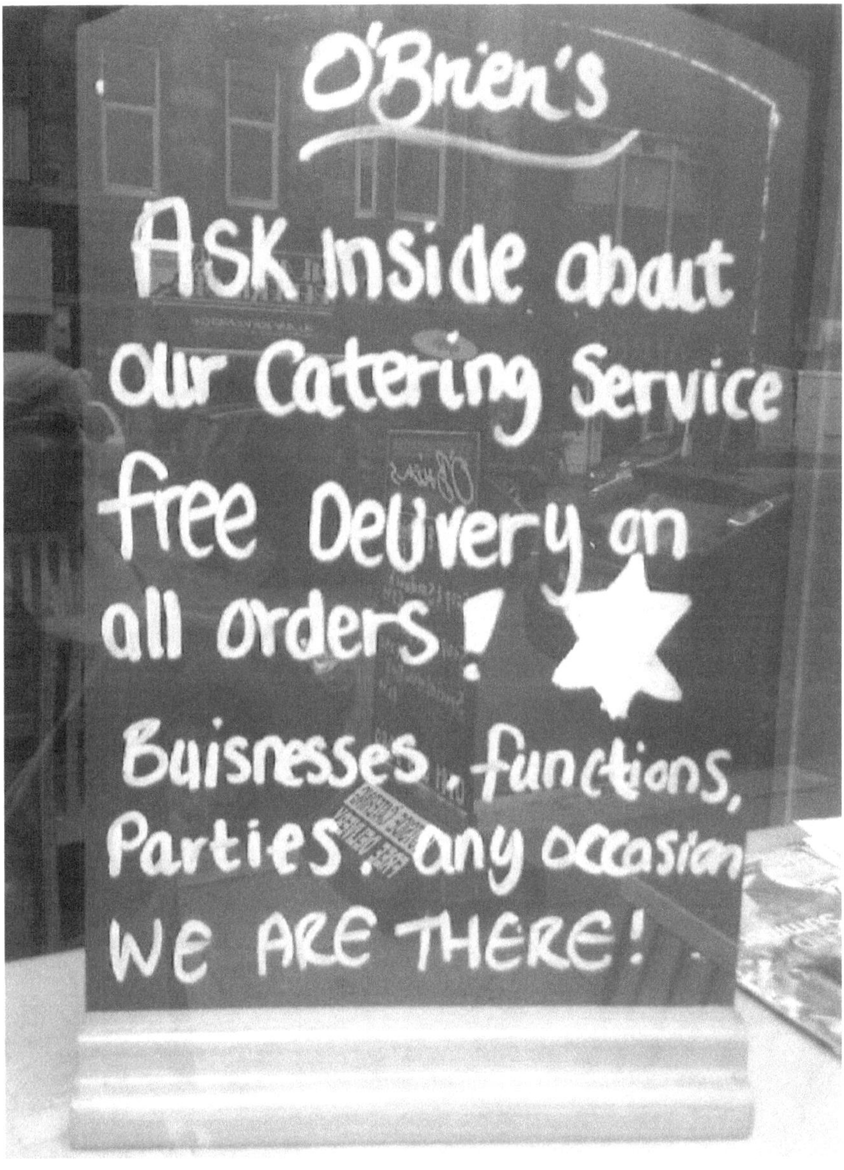
O'Brien's
Ask inside about our Catering Service
free Delivery on all orders!
Buisnesses, functions, Parties, any occasion
WE ARE THERE!

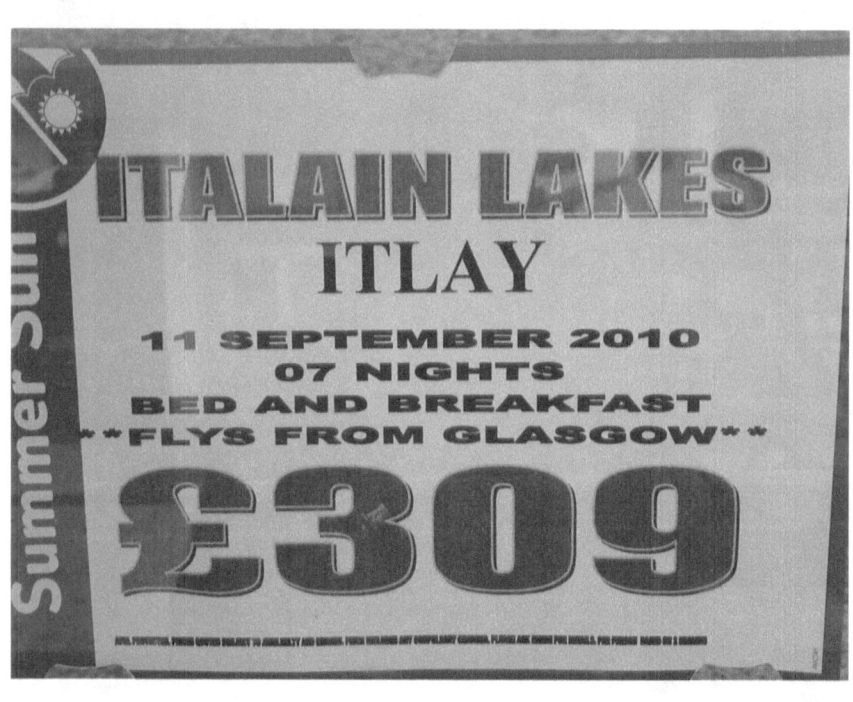

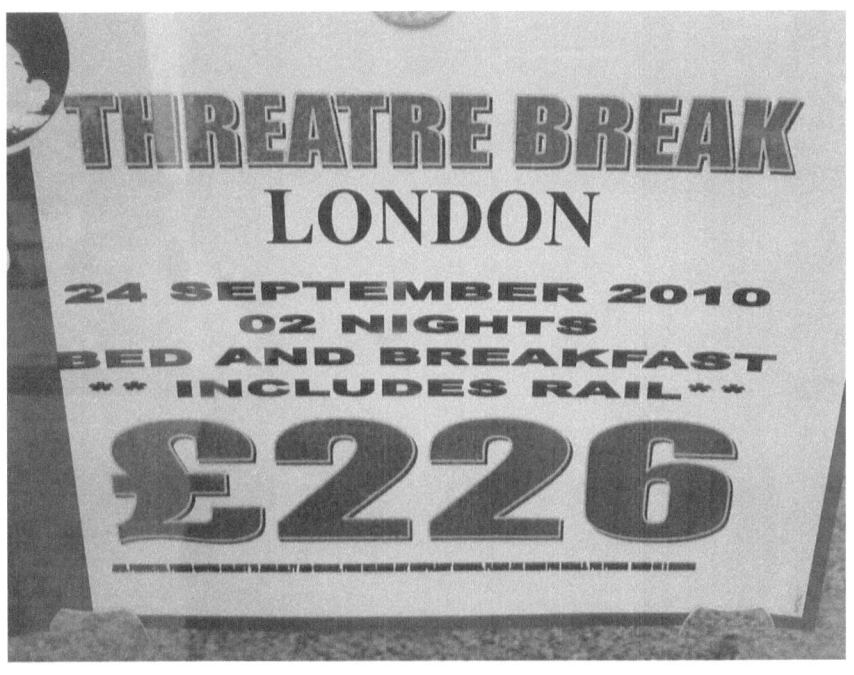

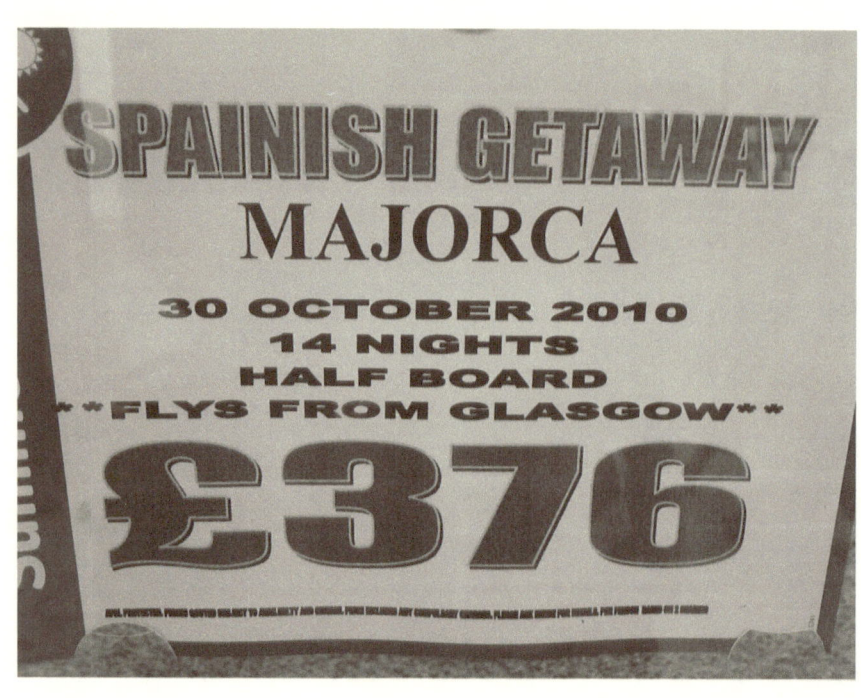

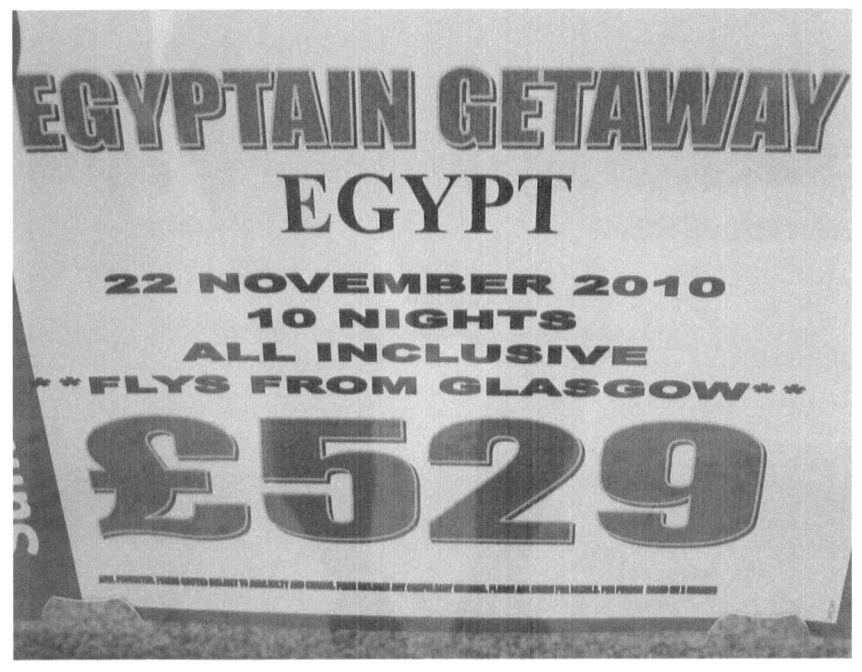

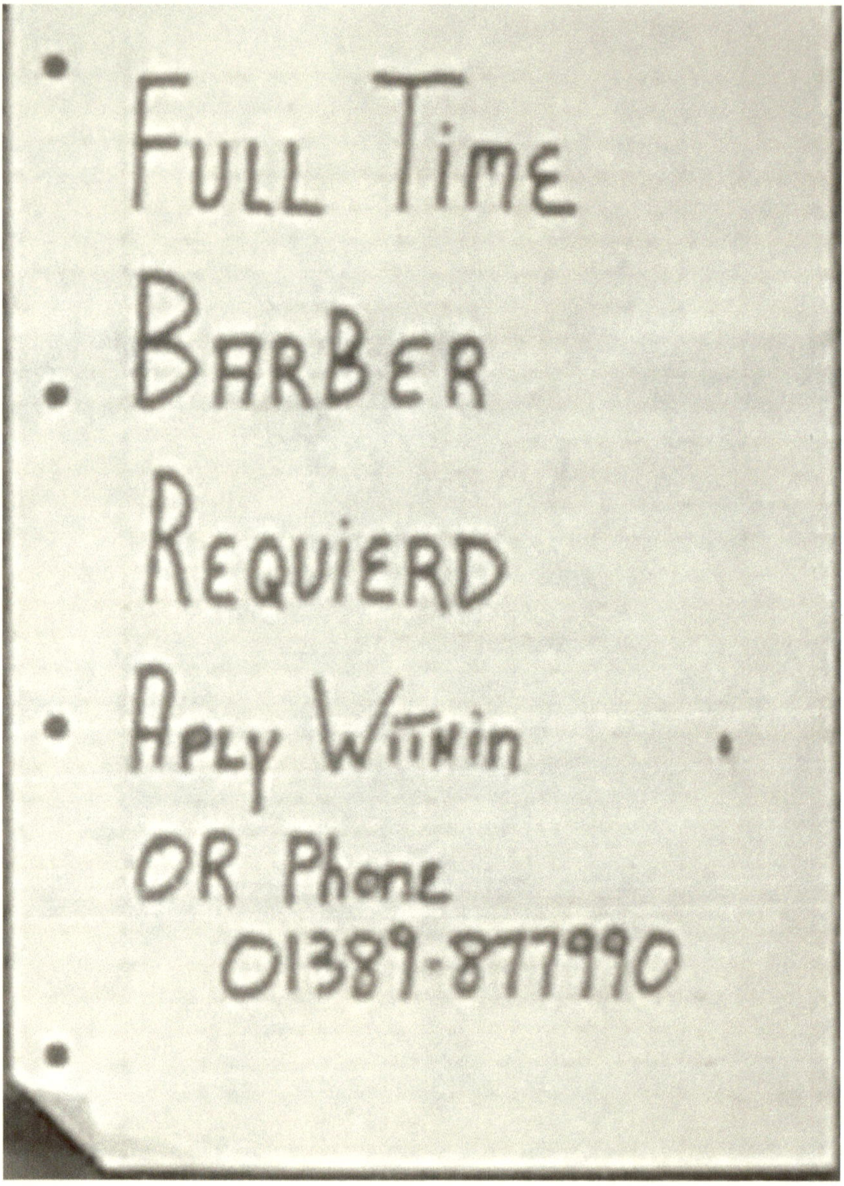

Full Time

Barber

Requierd

Aply Within

OR Phone

01389-877990

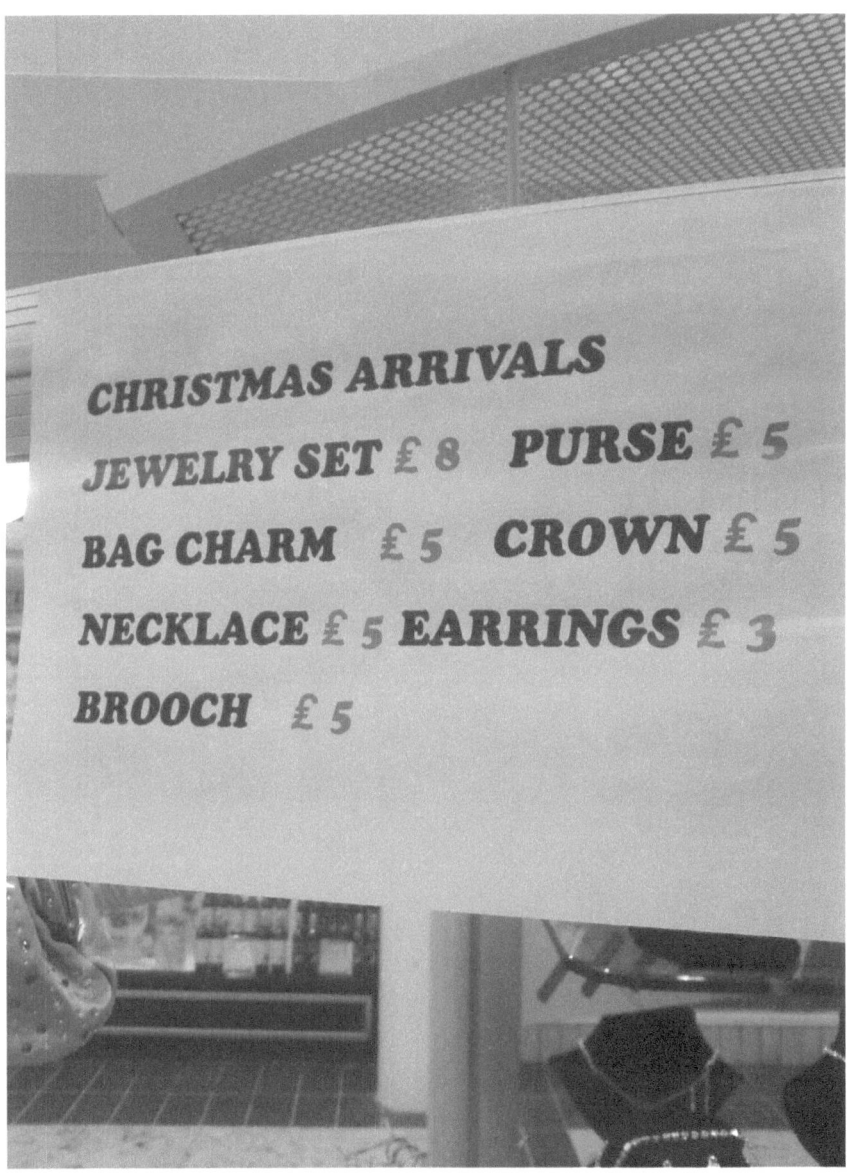

CHRISTMAS ARRIVALS

JEWELRY SET £ 8   PURSE £ 5

BAG CHARM £ 5   CROWN £ 5

NECKLACE £ 5 EARRINGS £ 3

BROOCH £ 5

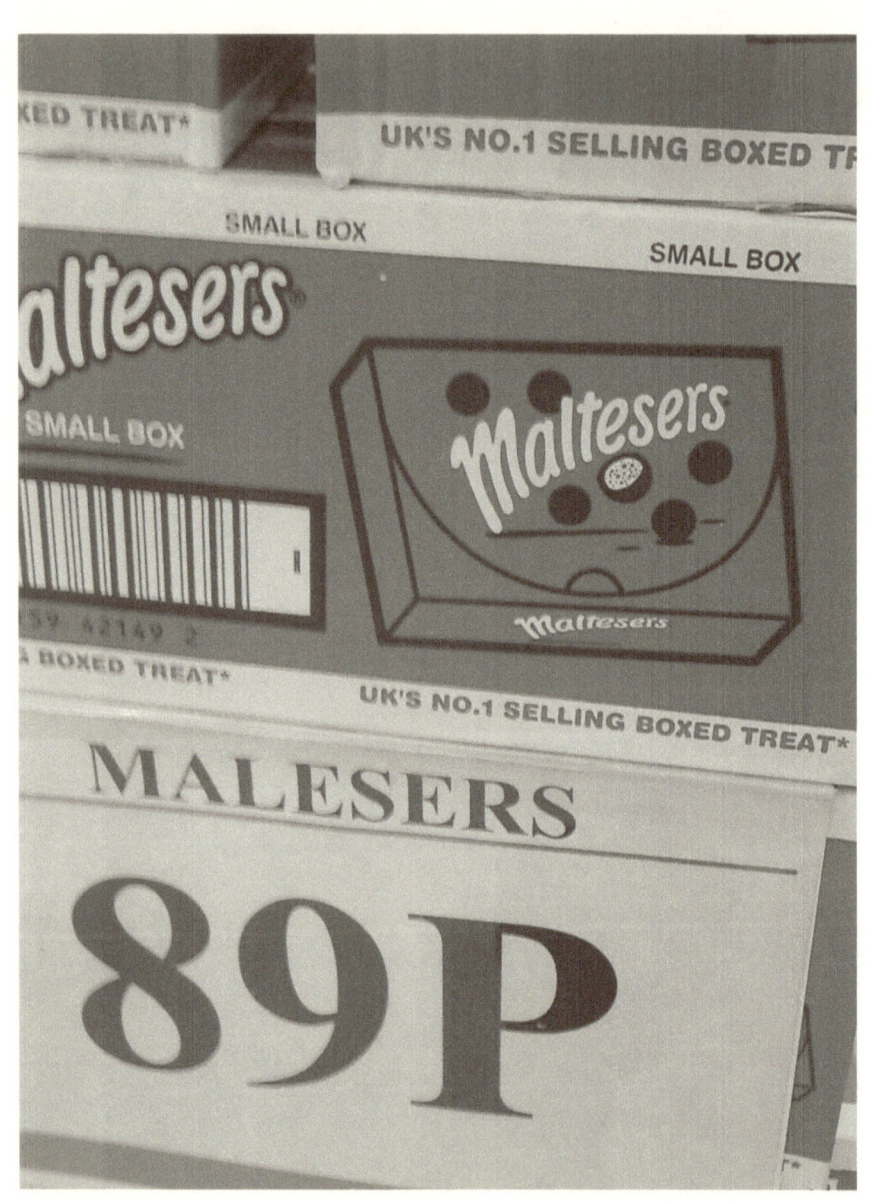

XED TREAT*

UK'S NO.1 SELLING BOXED TR

SMALL BOX

SMALL BOX

altesers®

SMALL BOX

59 42149 2

BOXED TREAT*

UK'S NO.1 SELLING BOXED TREAT*

MALESERS

89P

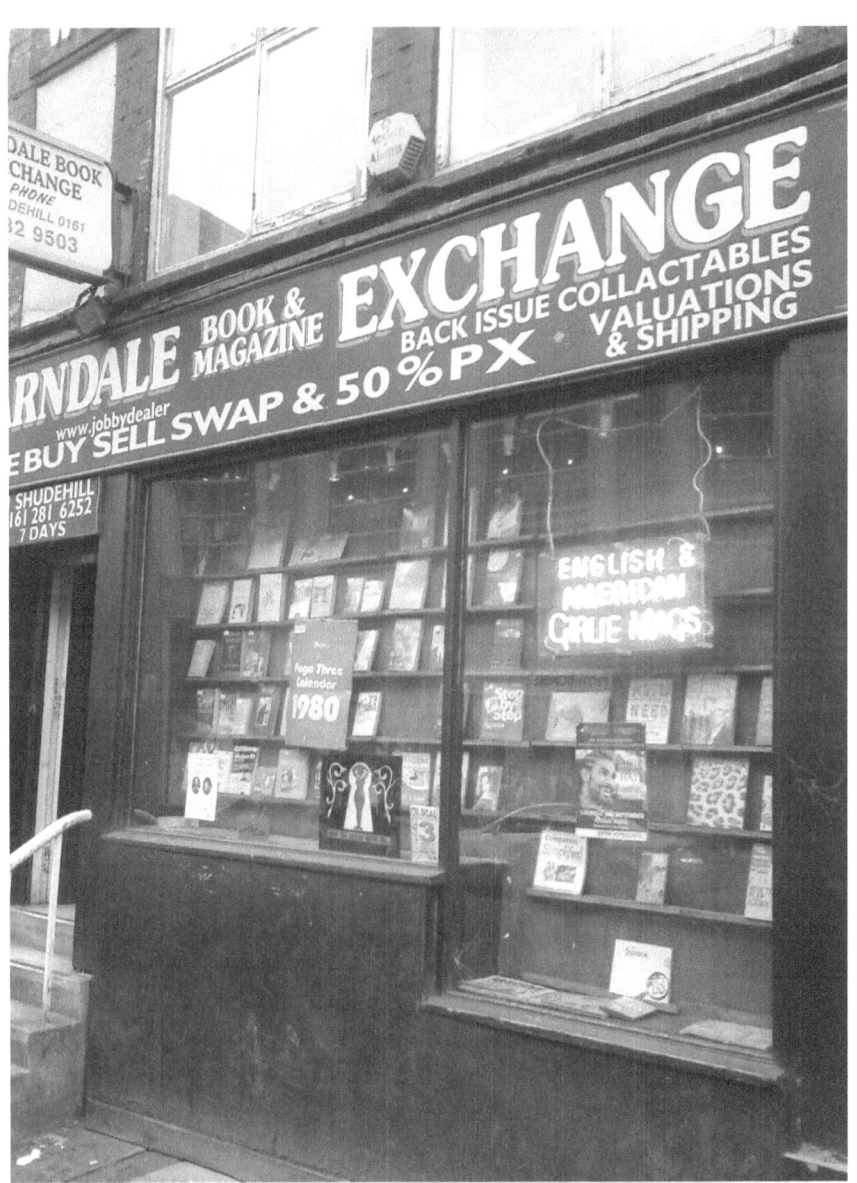

TELSTAR

HOGMANY

PARTY

3AM LICENCE

WITH LIVE MUSIC THROUGH THE BELLS WITH

ALAN CRANNEY

TICKETS ON SALE NEXT WEEK £5.00 ASK
STAFF FOR DETAILS (LIMITED AVAILABILITY)

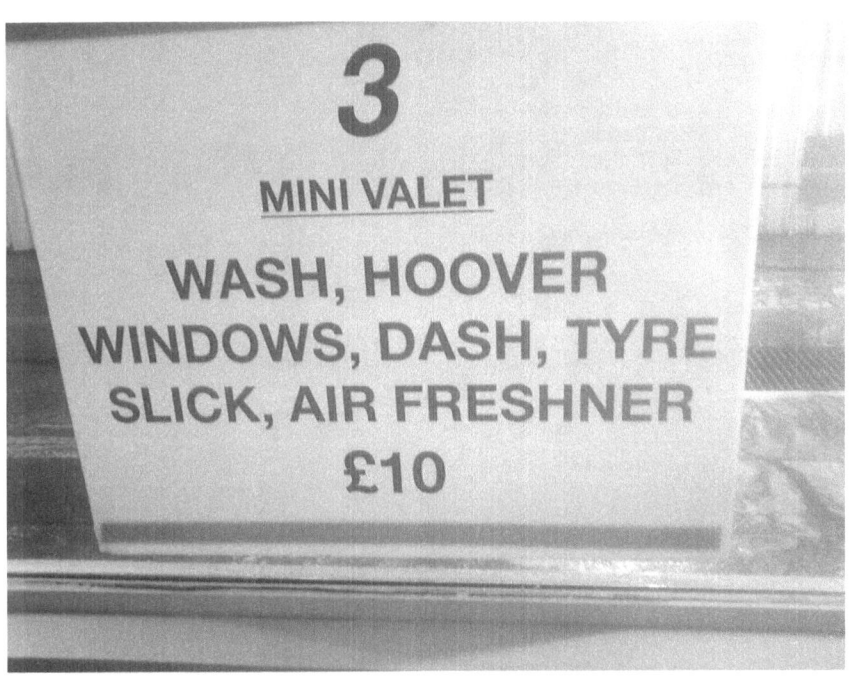

3

MINI VALET

WASH, HOOVER
WINDOWS, DASH, TYRE
SLICK, AIR FRESHNER
£10

OUT OF
ORDER

UNDER REPAIR

APOLGIES FOR ANY
INCONVENIENCE

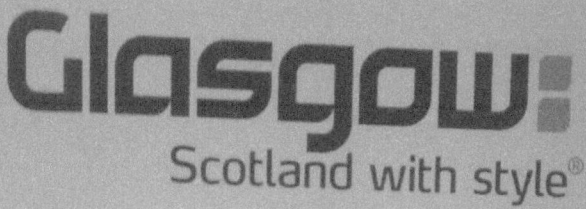

HASTE YE BACK

International Federation of Nurse Anesthetists

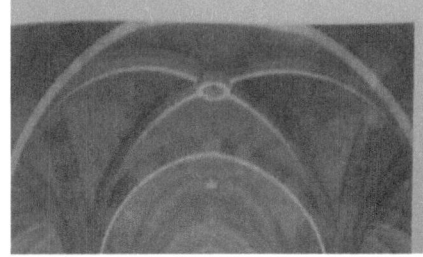 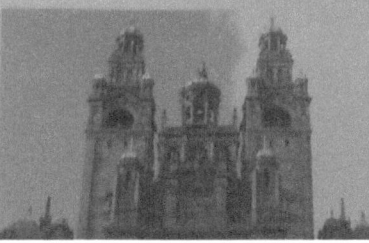

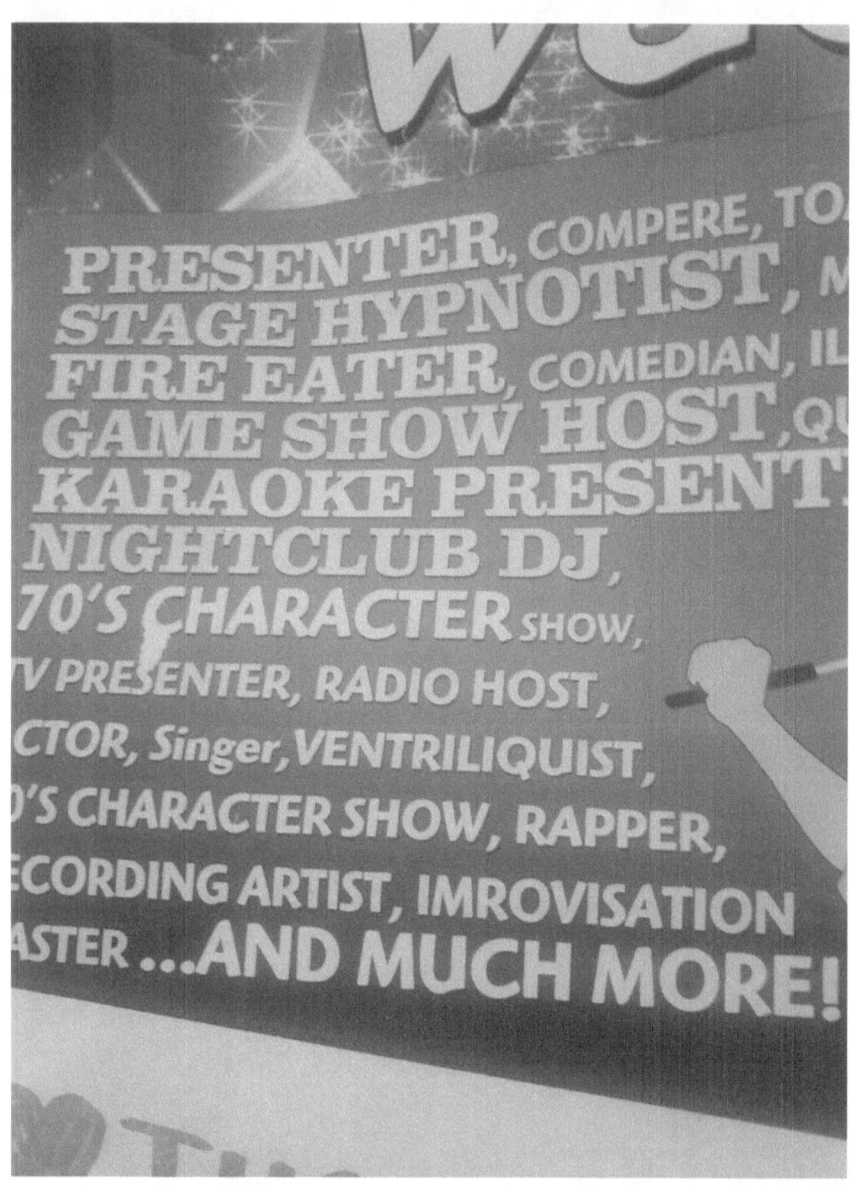

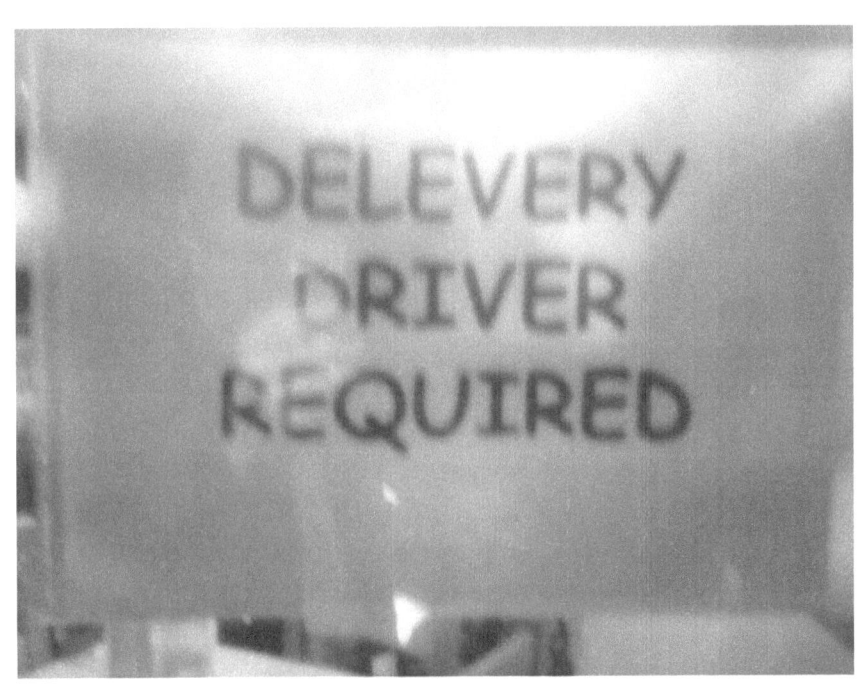

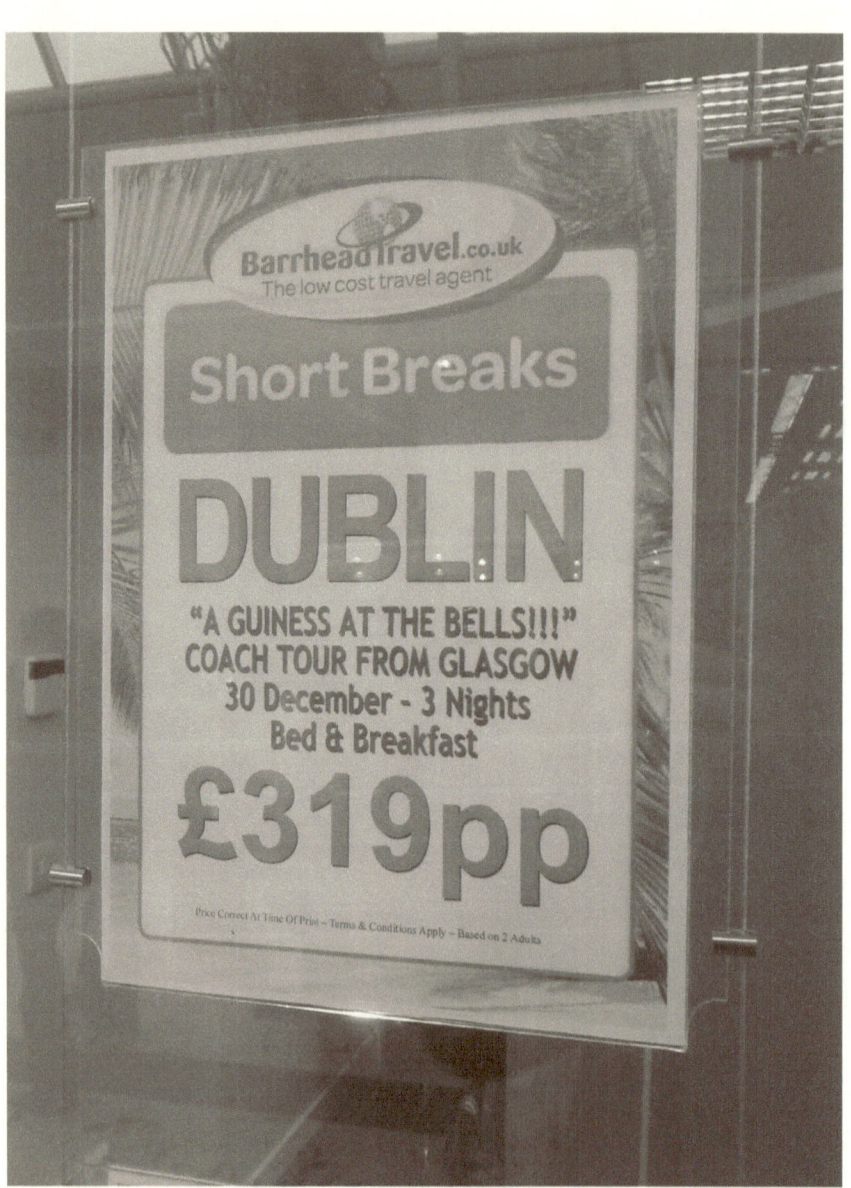

Breakfast Menu

★ Full Irish Breakfast
  - with tea/Coffee €7.95

NEW!! Fresh Waffels
  - Choice of topping full €3.50
                        ¼ 99c

★ Selection of Cereal,
   Pastries, Muffins,
   Jumb Scones......

JUST WEIRD

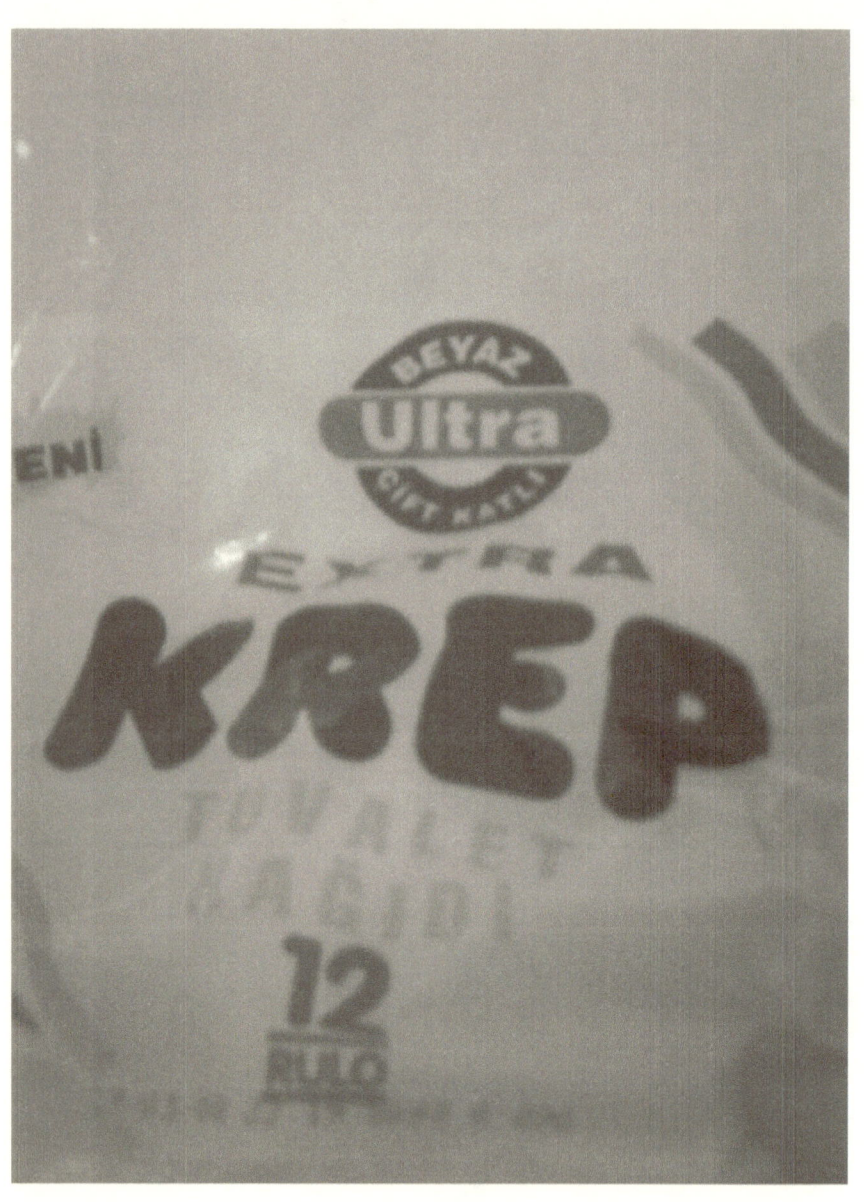

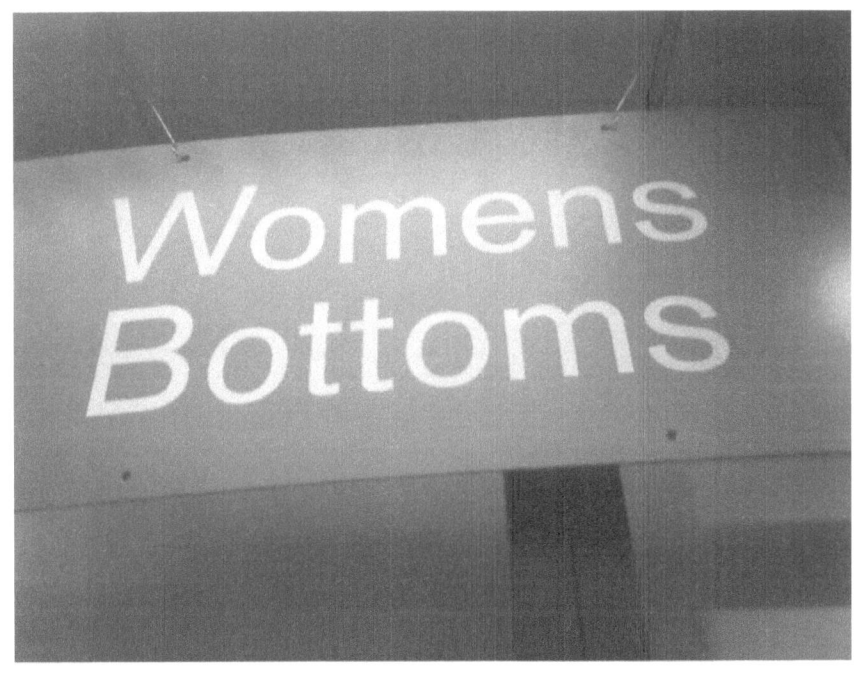

72

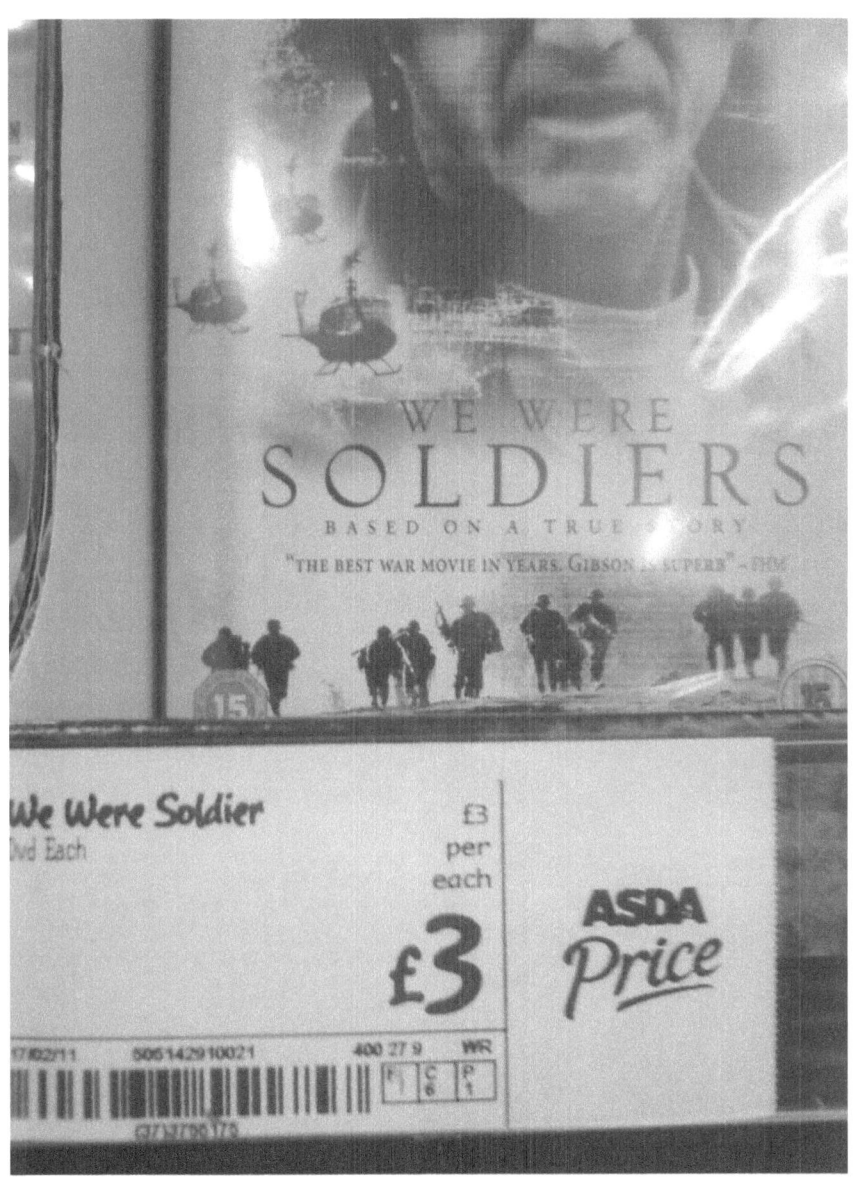

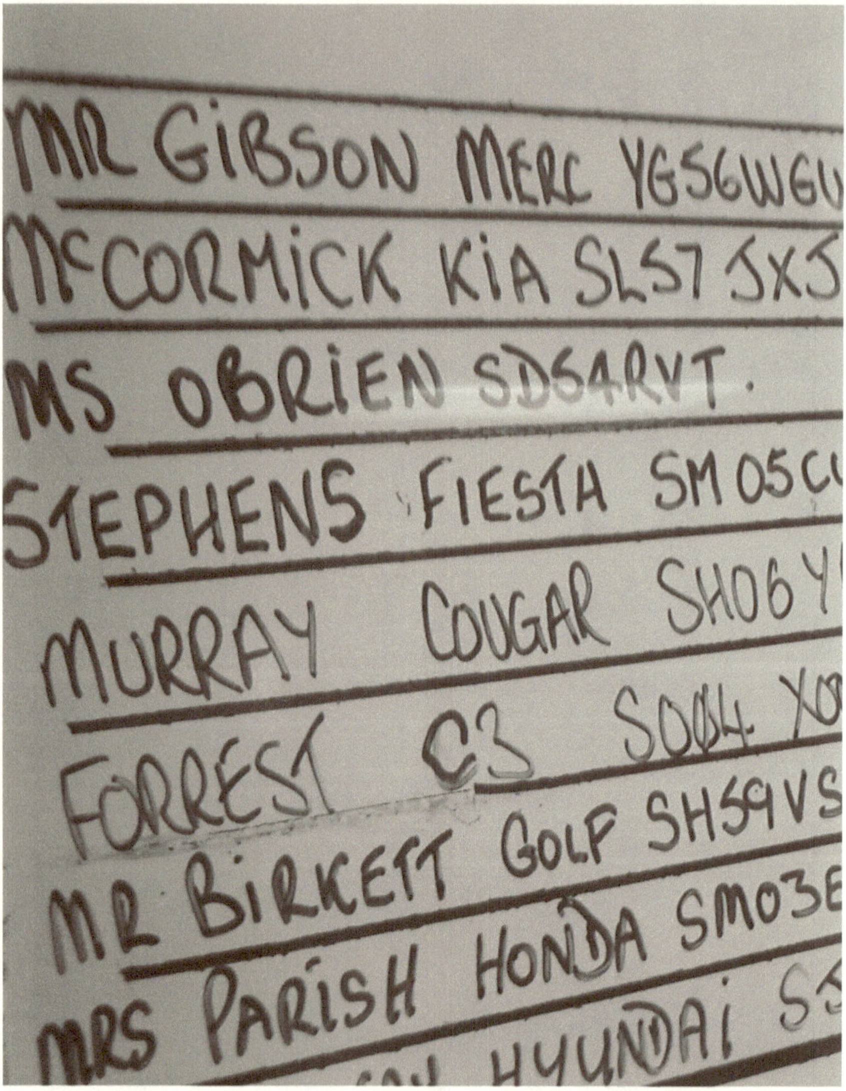

MR GIBSON MERC YG56WGU

MCCORMICK KIA SL57 JX5

MS OBRIEN SD54RVT.

STEPHENS FIESTA SM05C

MURRAY COUGAR SH06Y

FORREST C3 SO04 XO

MR BIRKETT GOLF SH59VS

MRS PARISH HONDA SM03E

HYUNDAI S5

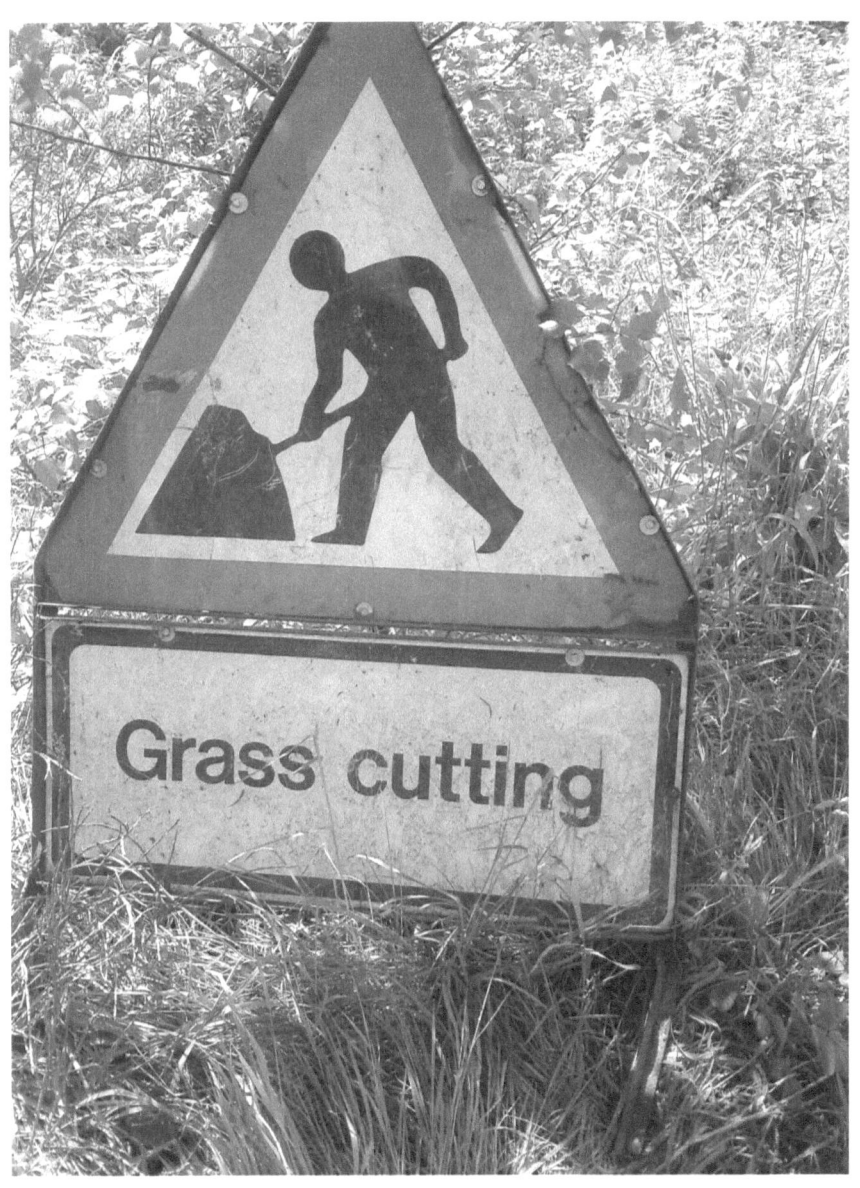

THESE TOILETS ARE CHECKED EVERY 115 MINUTES

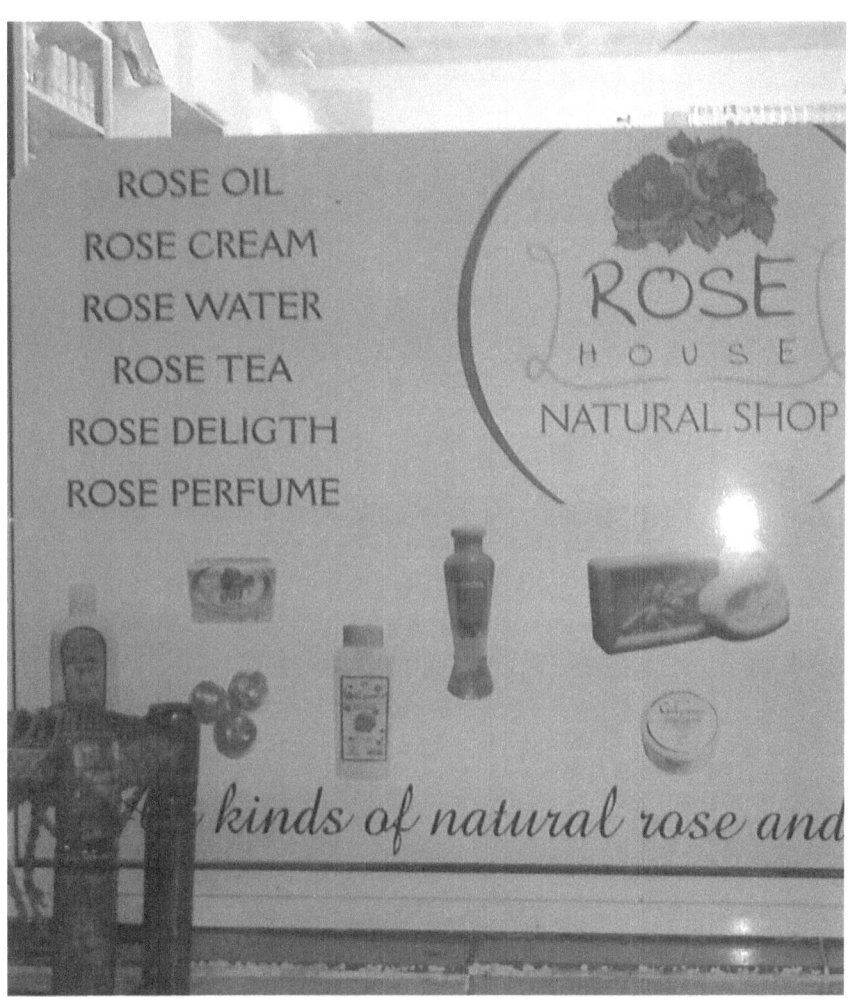

ROSE OIL
ROSE CREAM
ROSE WATER
ROSE TEA
ROSE DELIGTH
ROSE PERFUME

ROSE
H O U S E
NATURAL SHOP

kinds of natural rose and

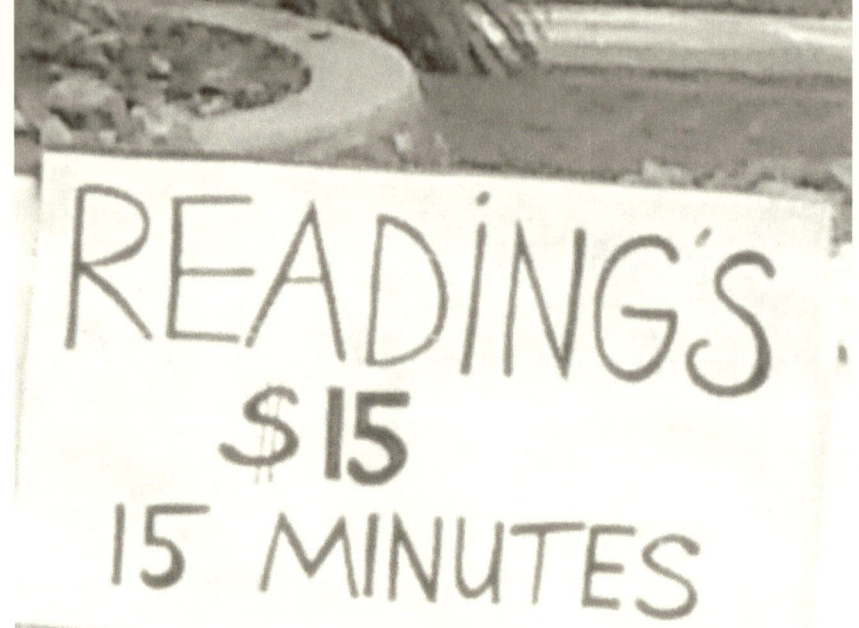

READING'S
$15
15 MINUTES

REIKI
HEALING

INSIDE BOOKSHOP

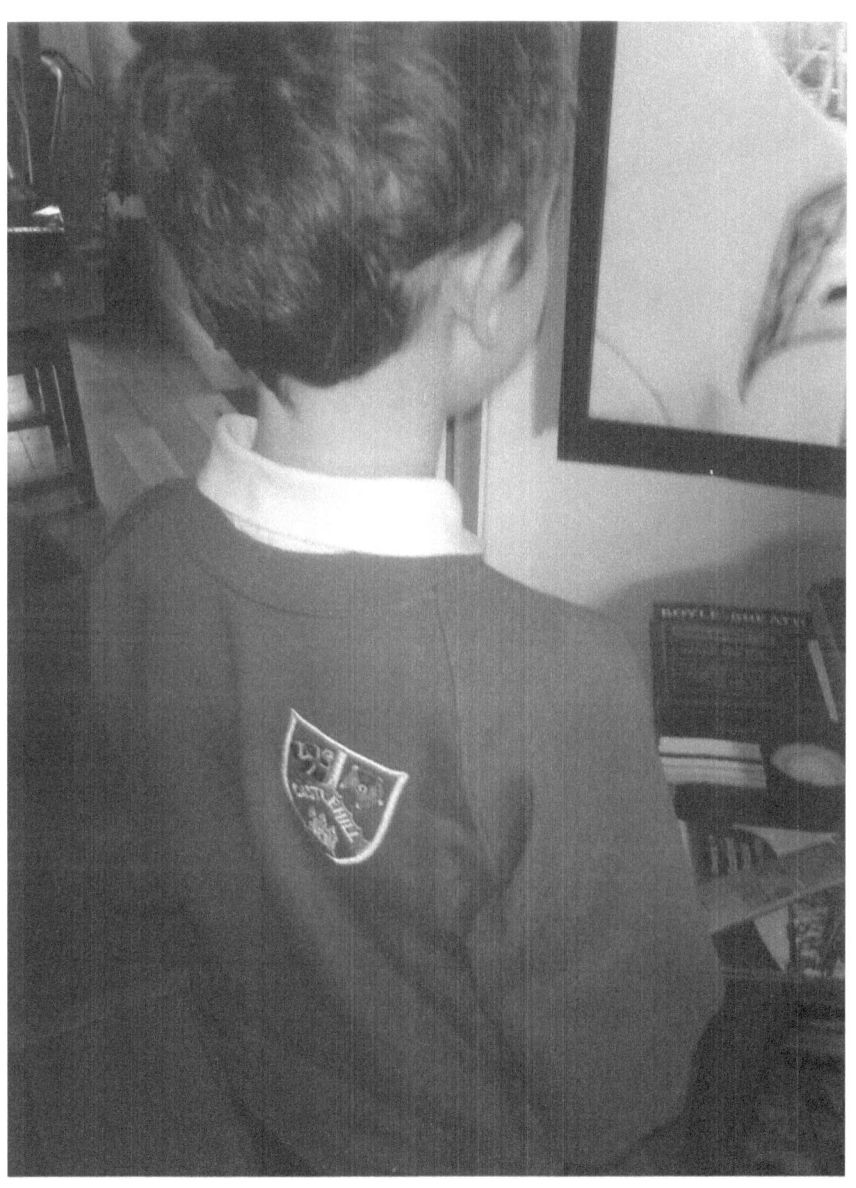

OUT
OF
ORDER

Please either use the disabled toilet

Or the baby changing room toilet

Sorry for any inconvenience

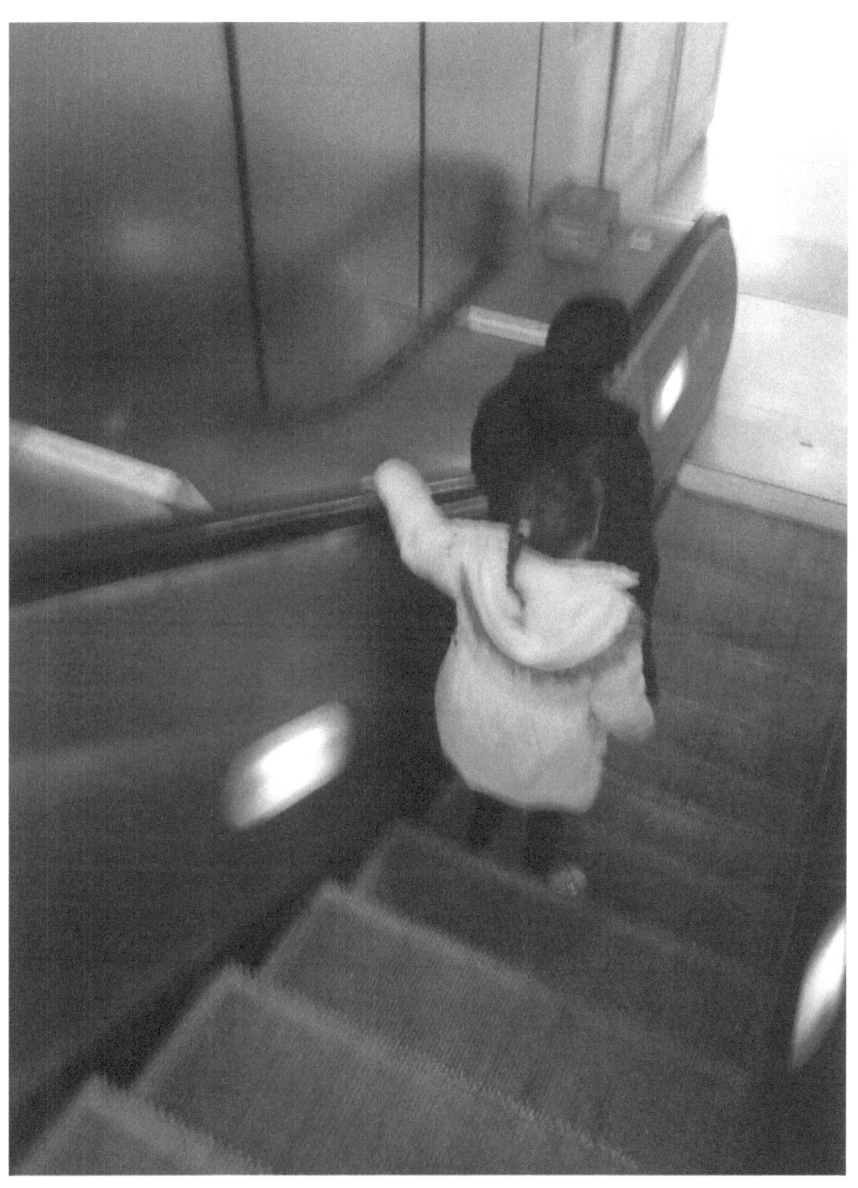

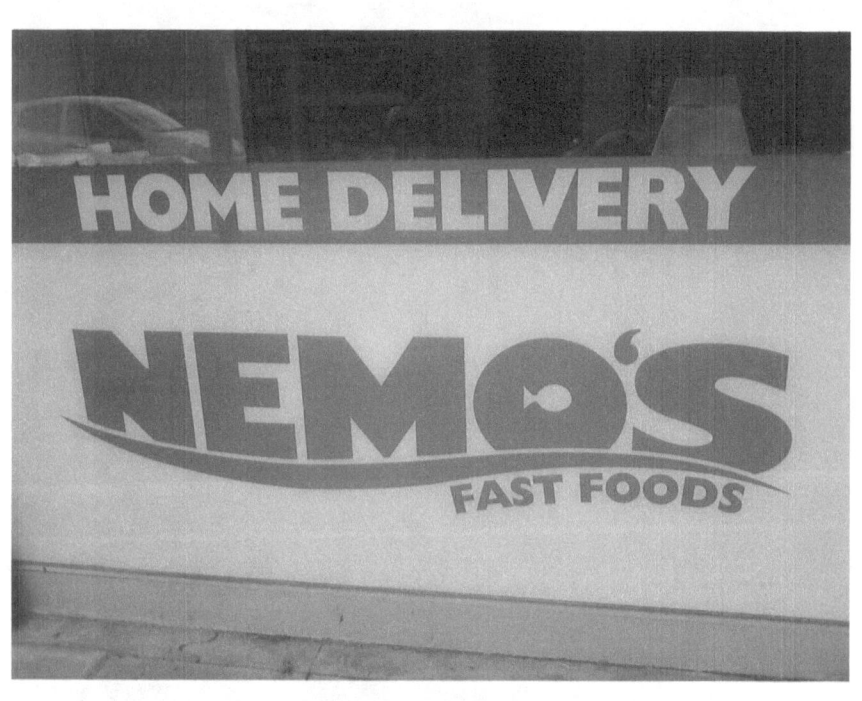

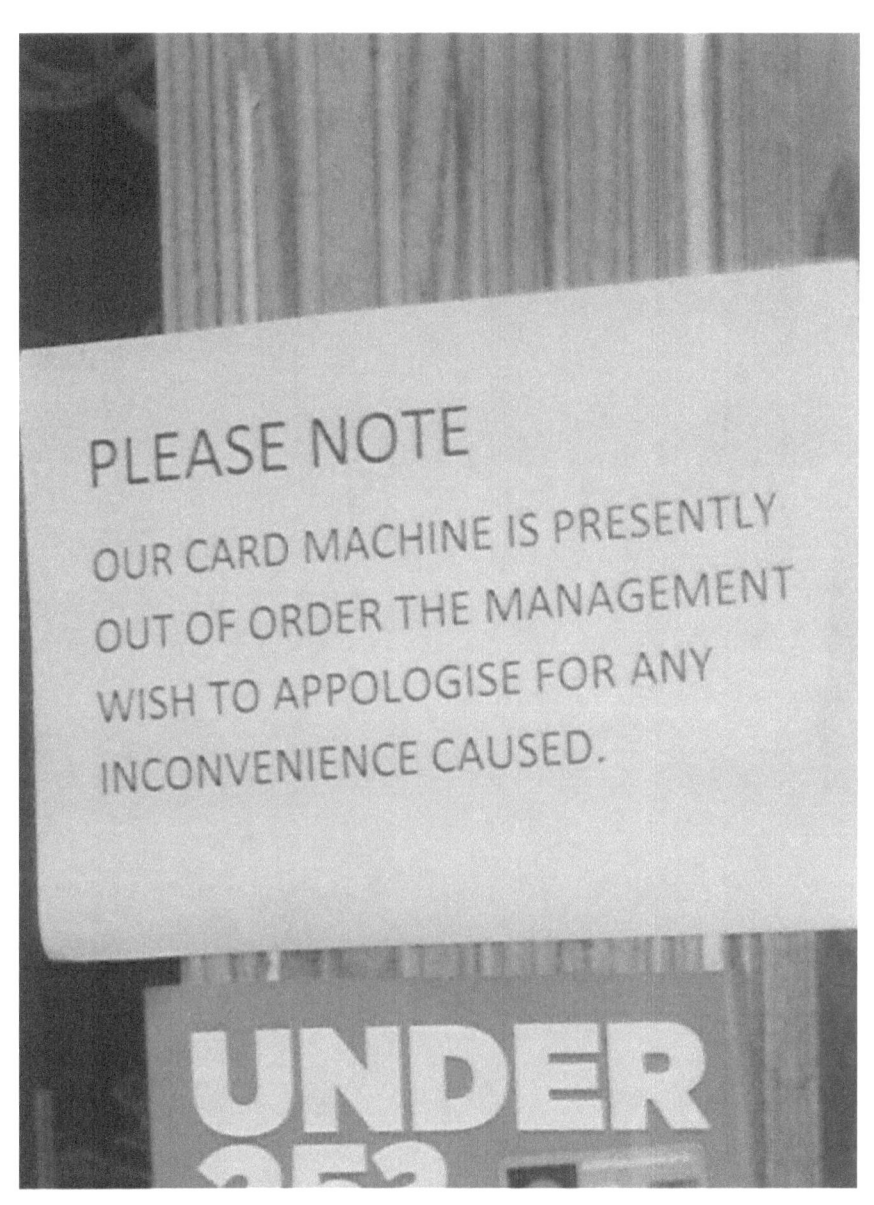

PLEASE NOTE

OUR CARD MACHINE IS PRESENTLY
OUT OF ORDER THE MANAGEMENT
WISH TO APPOLOGISE FOR ANY
INCONVENIENCE CAUSED.

UNDER

EDINBURGH GHOST TOUR

INCUDING UNDERGROUND VAULT

A tour round the dark and most haunted streets of Edinburgh's world famous Roya mile. Terrifying tales of: Ghosts, Hangings Torture, Murders and Witchcraft. Are you brave enough to venture into Edinburgh's dark past!

19.15 (7.15

AUSTRALIA - MAY 2013

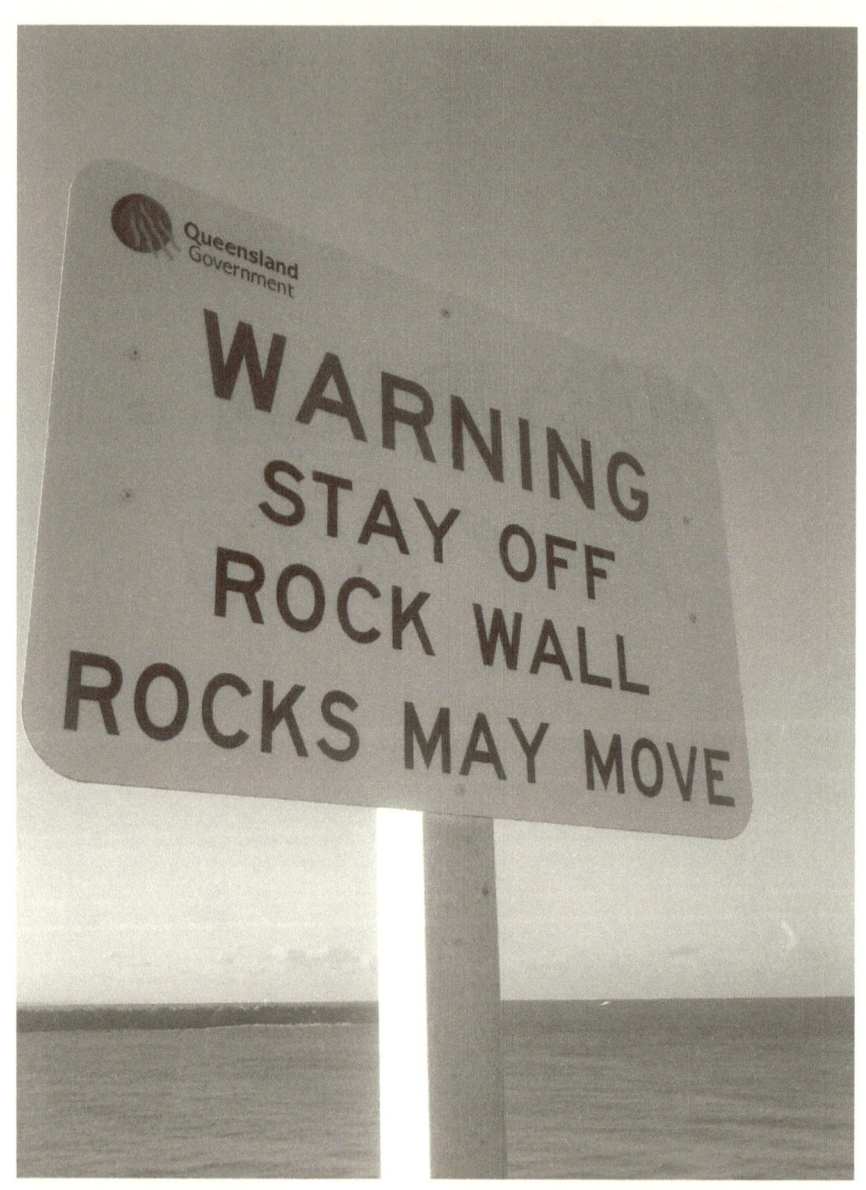

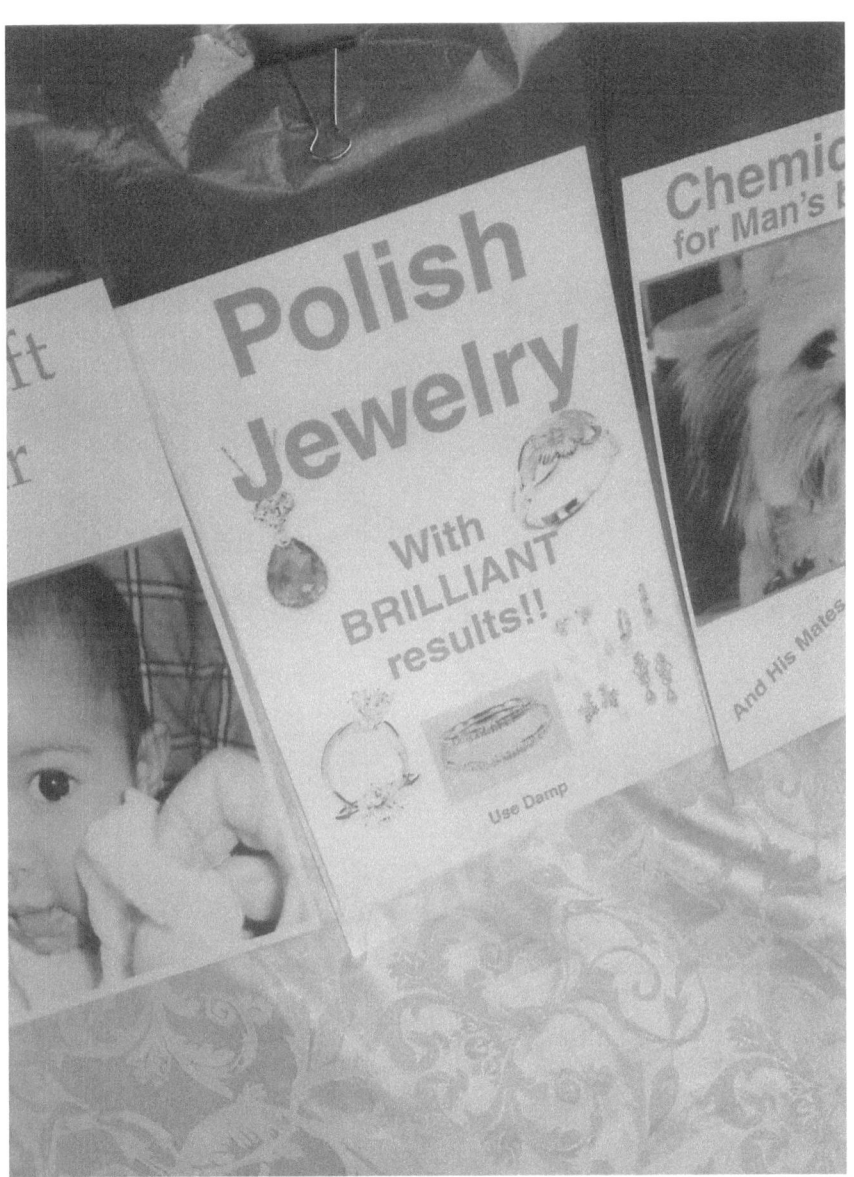

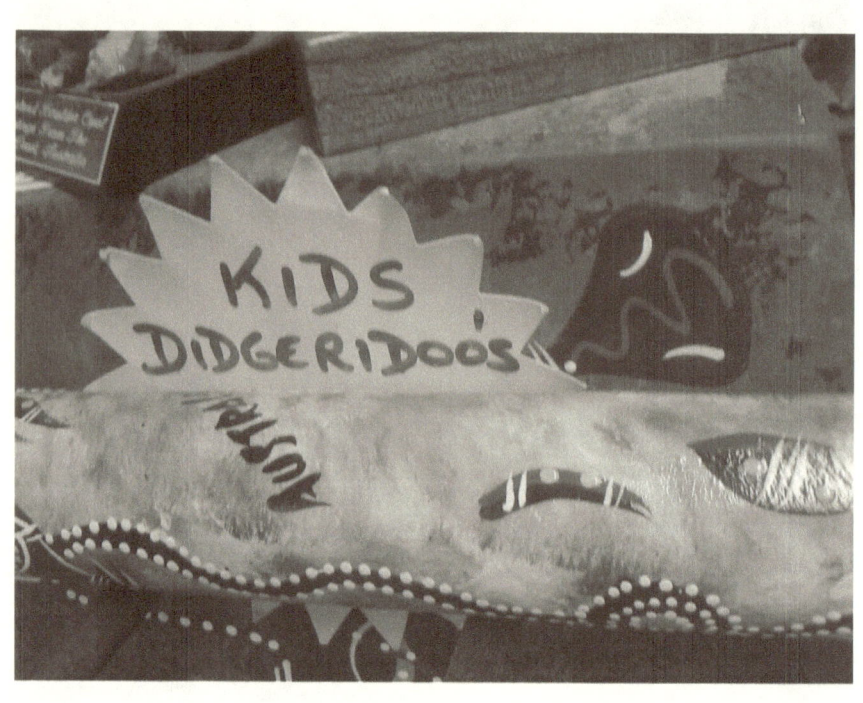

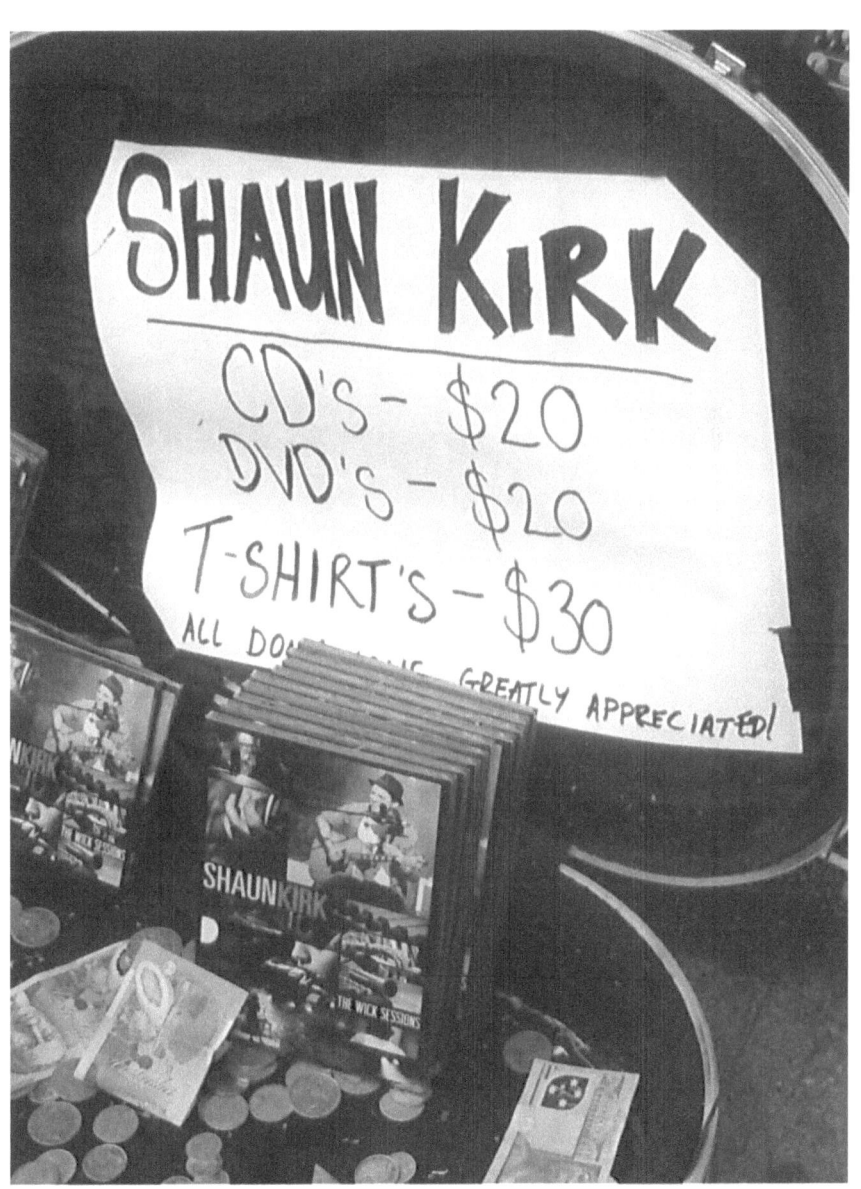

ONLY RIGHT
SHOE ON
TABLE

**Please ask staff for assistance to
try complete pair**

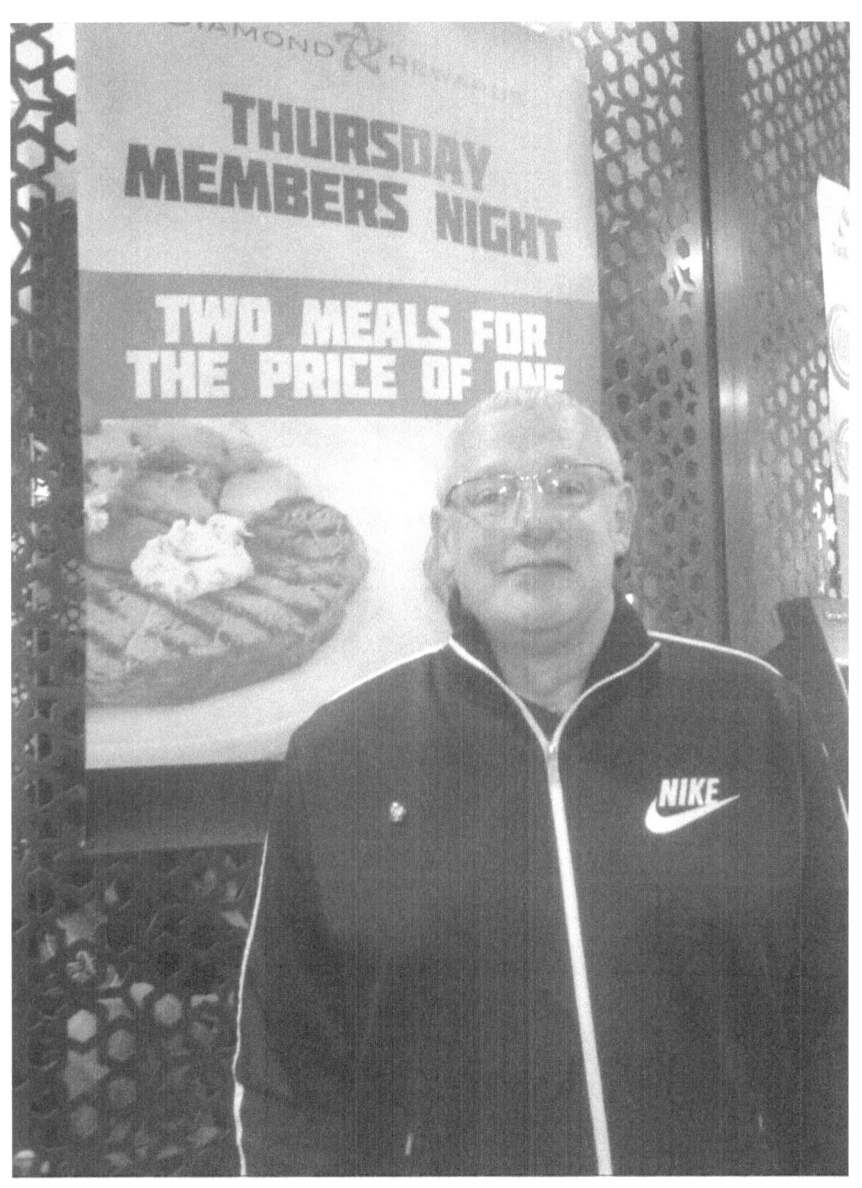

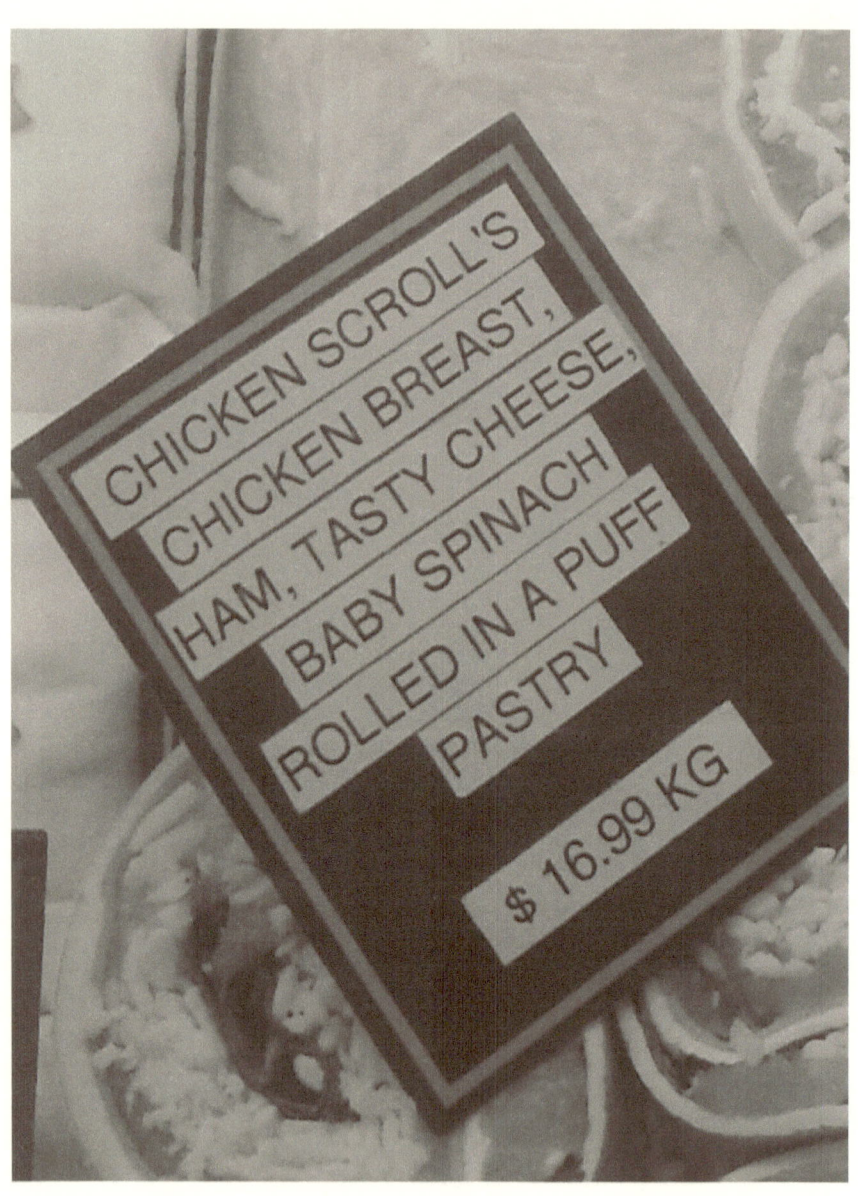

CHICKEN SCROLL'S
CHICKEN BREAST,
HAM, TASTY CHEESE,
BABY SPINACH
ROLLED IN A PUFF
PASTRY

$ 16.99 KG

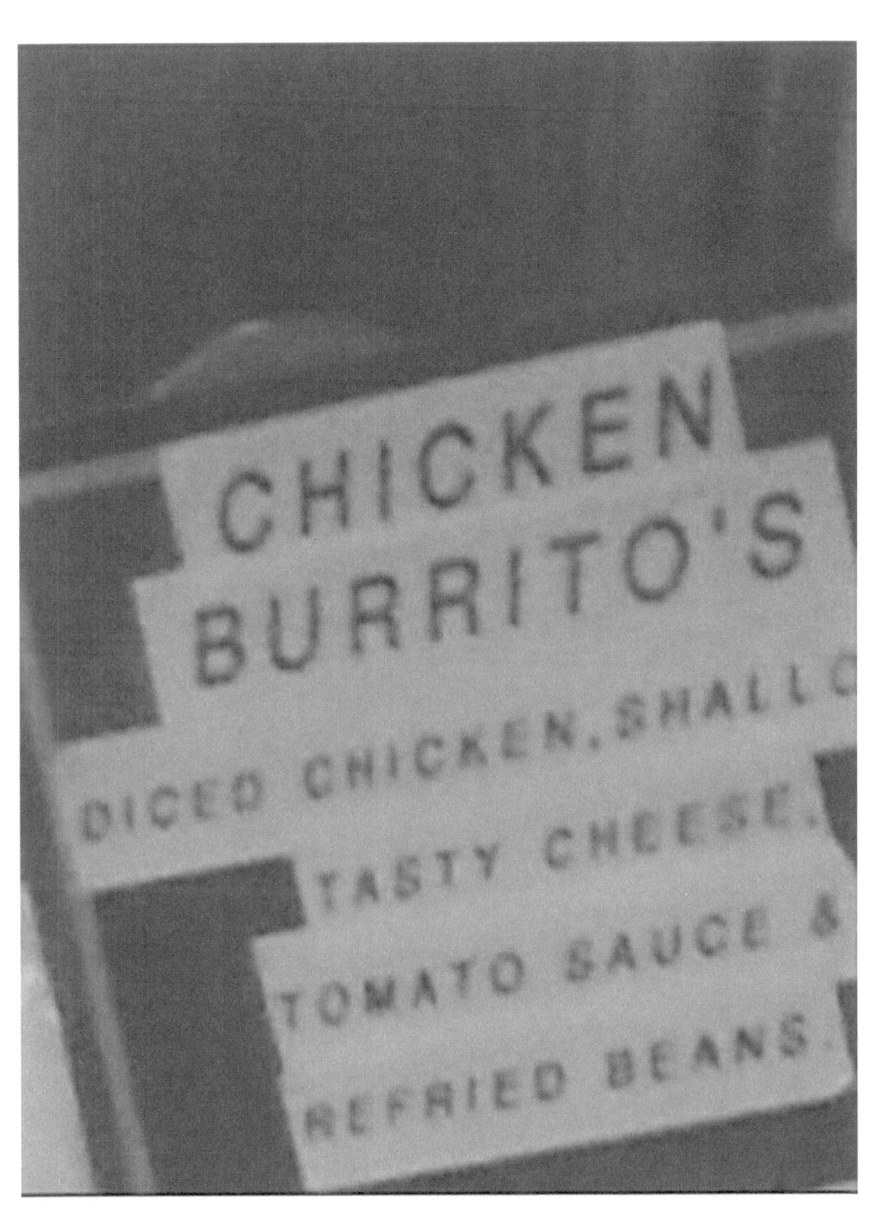

CHICKEN
BURRITO'S

DICED CHICKEN, SHALLO
TASTY CHEESE,
TOMATO SAUCE &
REFRIED BEANS.

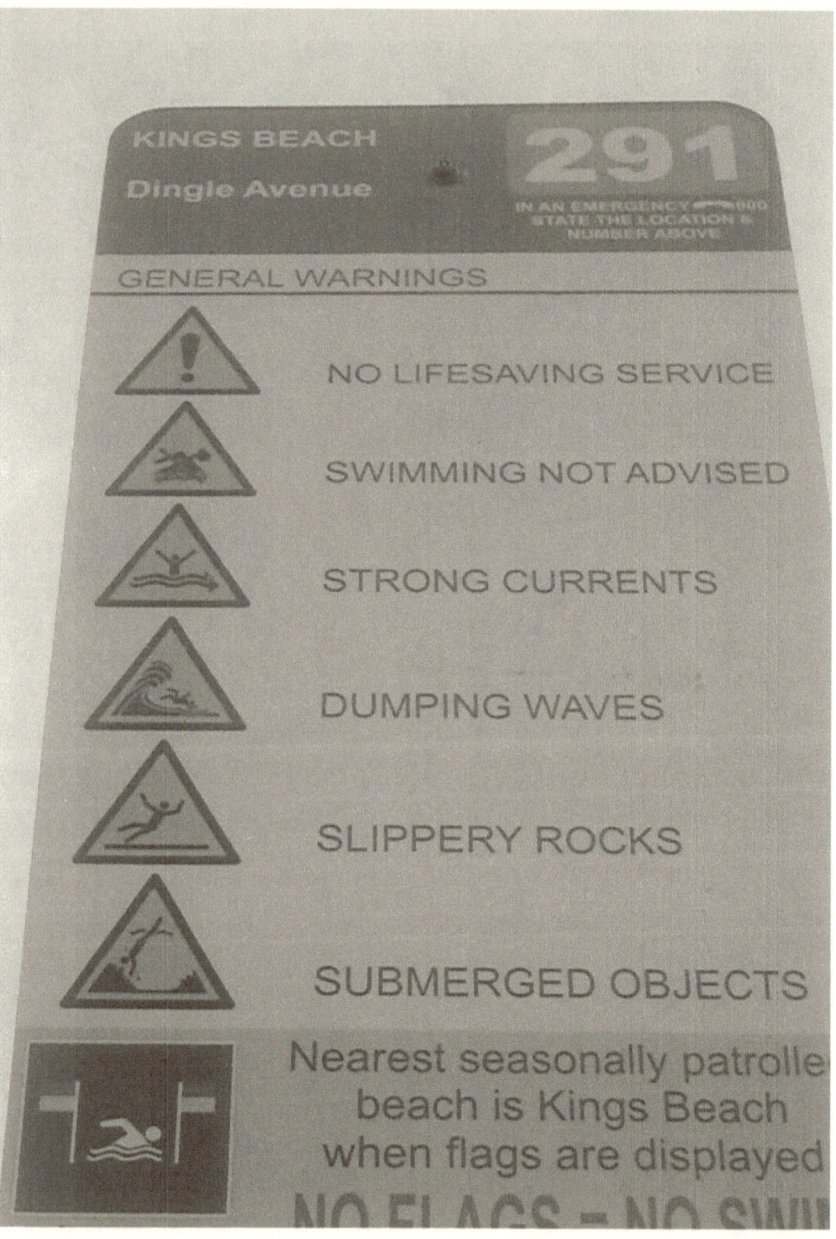

KINGS BEACH

Dingle Avenue

291

IN AN EMERGENCY ☎ 000
STATE THE LOCATION &
NUMBER ABOVE

GENERAL WARNINGS

NO LIFESAVING SERVICE

SWIMMING NOT ADVISED

STRONG CURRENTS

DUMPING WAVES

SLIPPERY ROCKS

SUBMERGED OBJECTS

Nearest seasonally patrolle
beach is Kings Beach
when flags are displayed

NO FLAGS – NO SWI

94

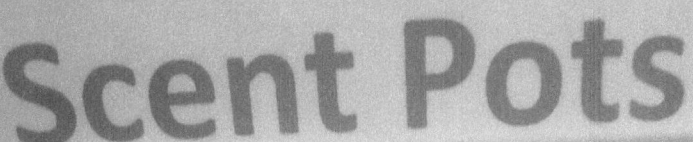

Scent Pots

Fill your scent pots with three to four drops of 100% Australian Eucalyptus Oil (or any other of your favourite oil's). The Banksia will soak up the oil and fragrance your room for weeks!

They are a great freshener for your bathroom, bedroom or wardrobe!

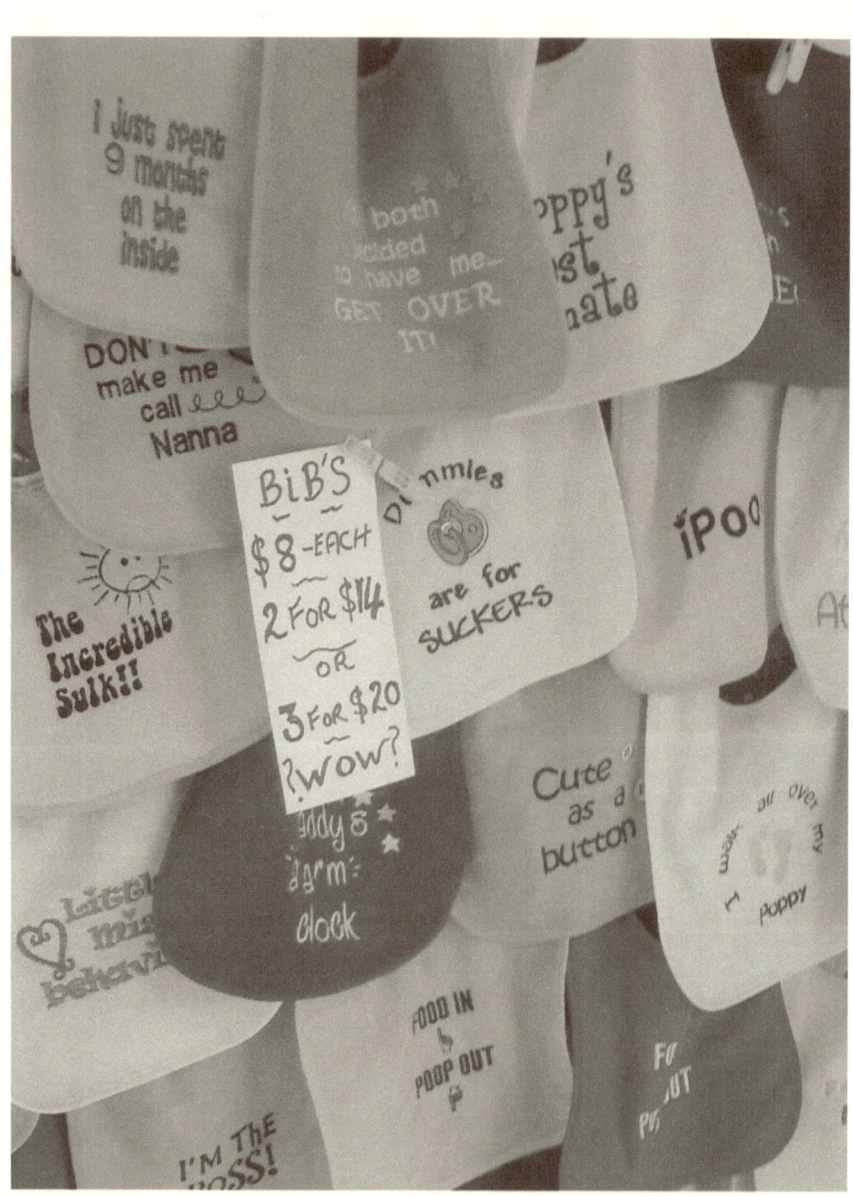

FOREIGN ERRORS?!

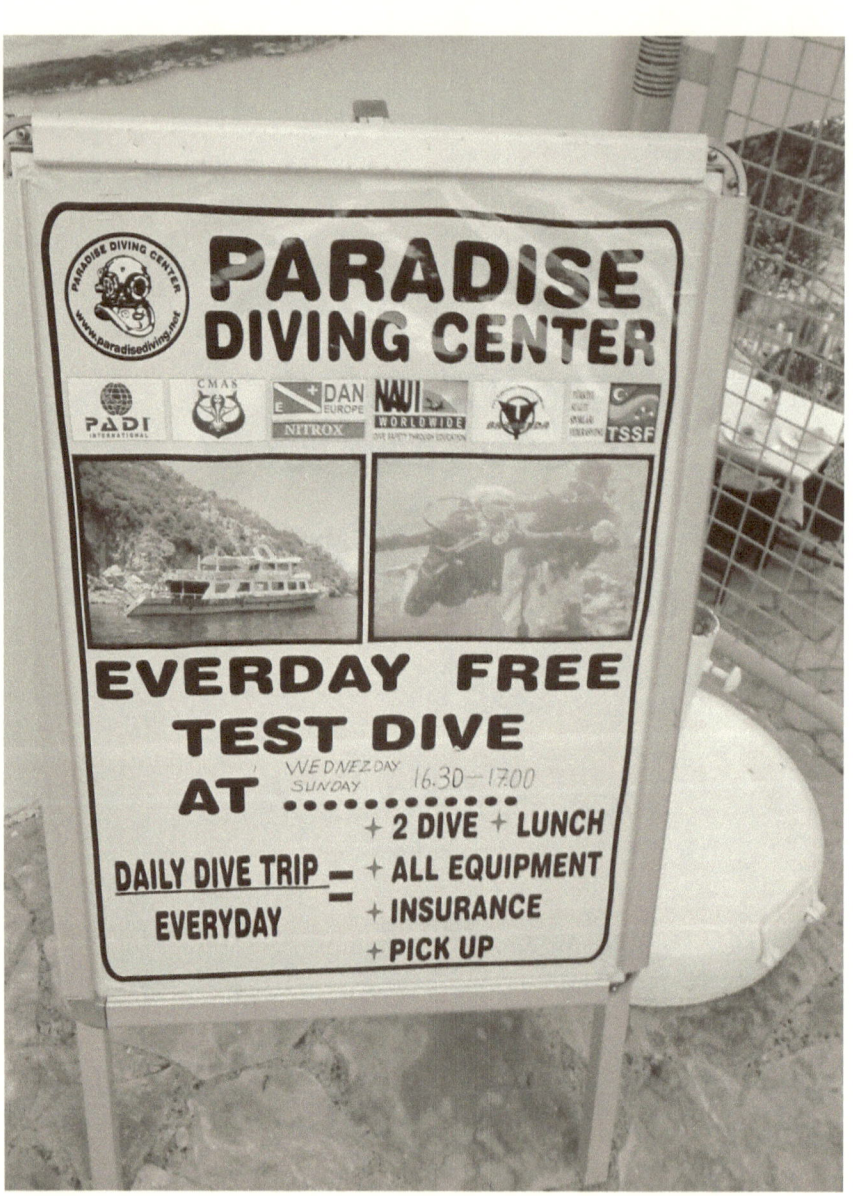

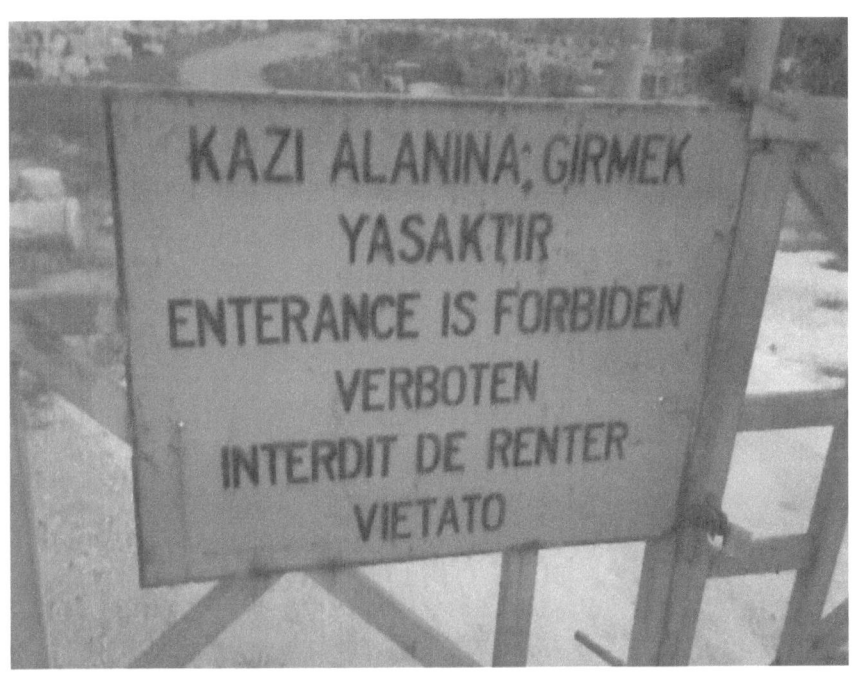

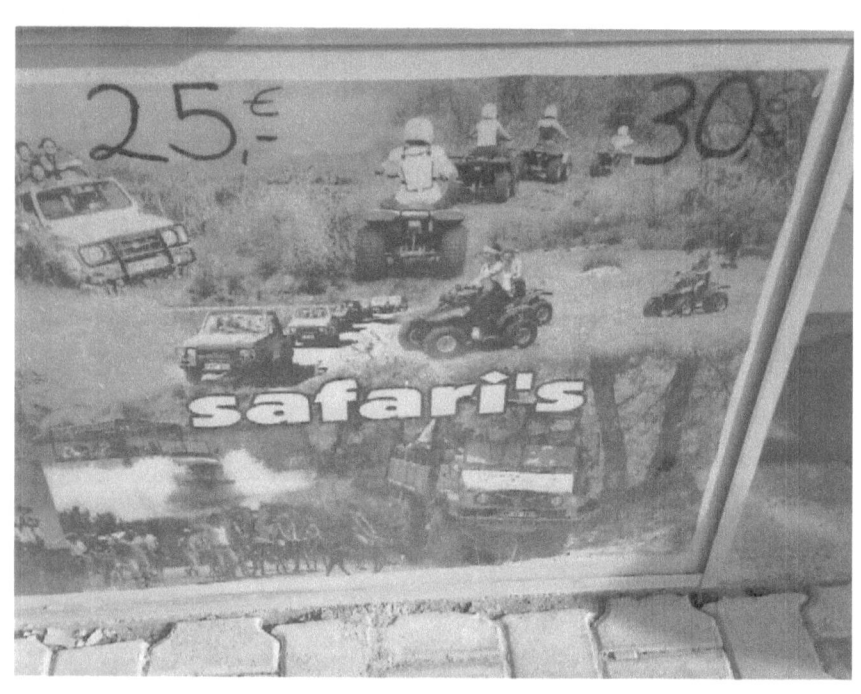

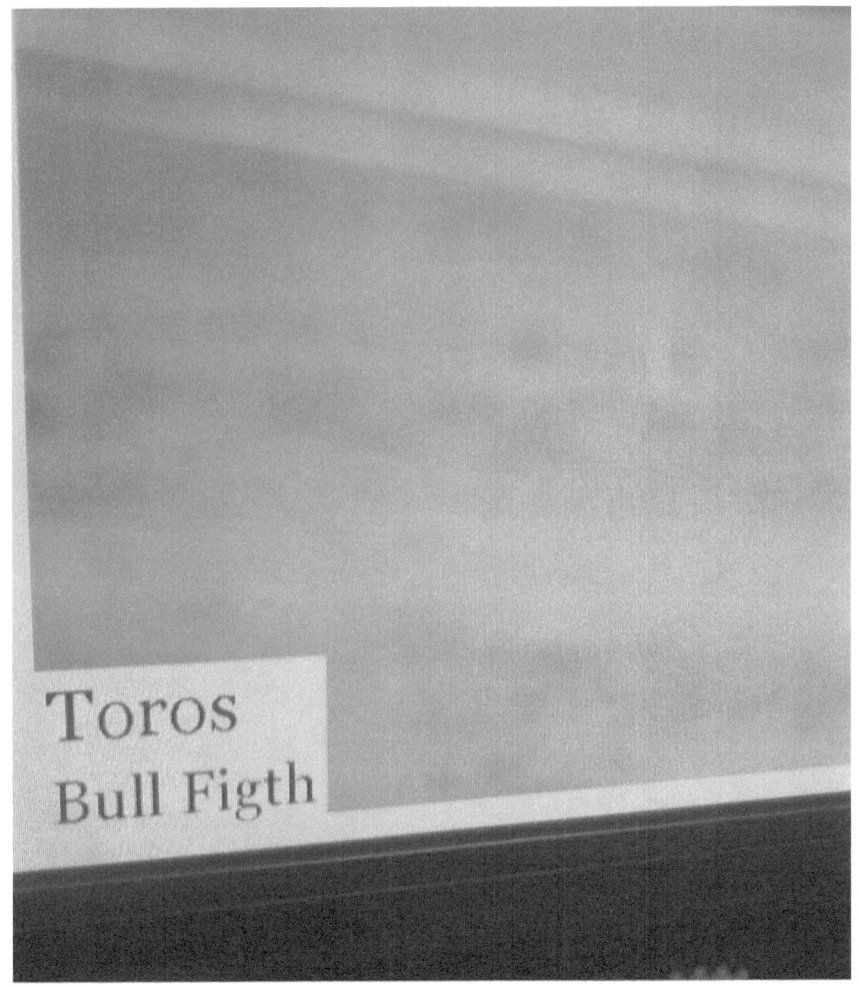

Toros
Bull Figth

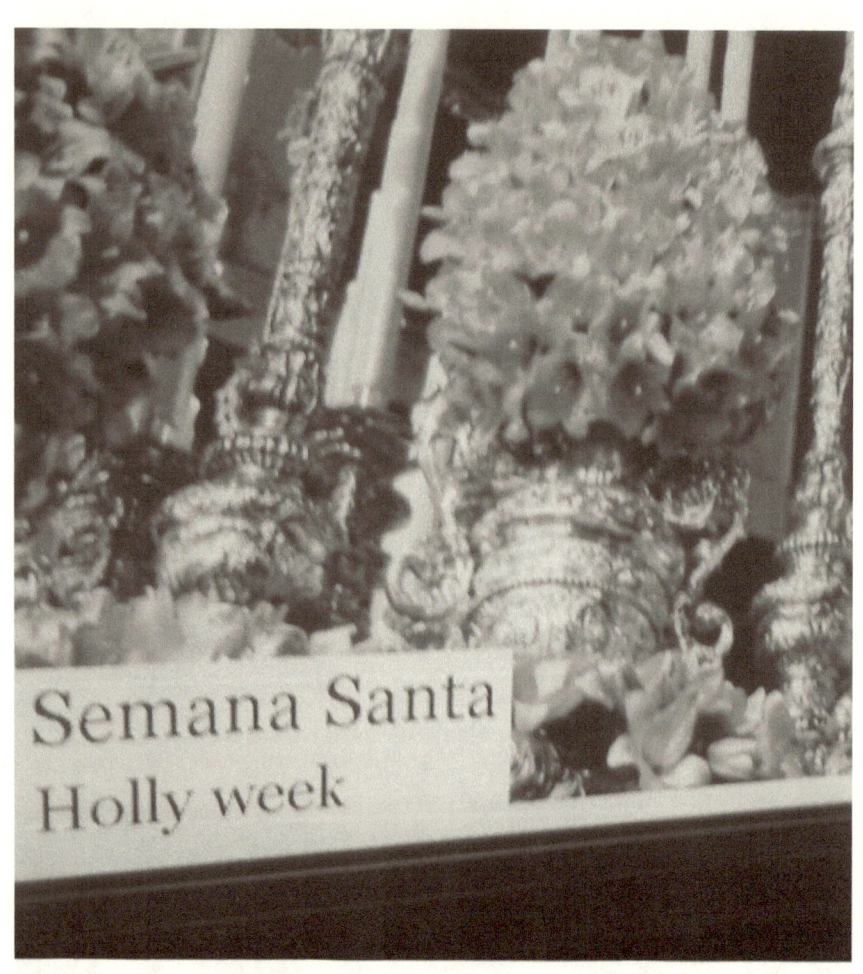

Semana Santa
Holly week

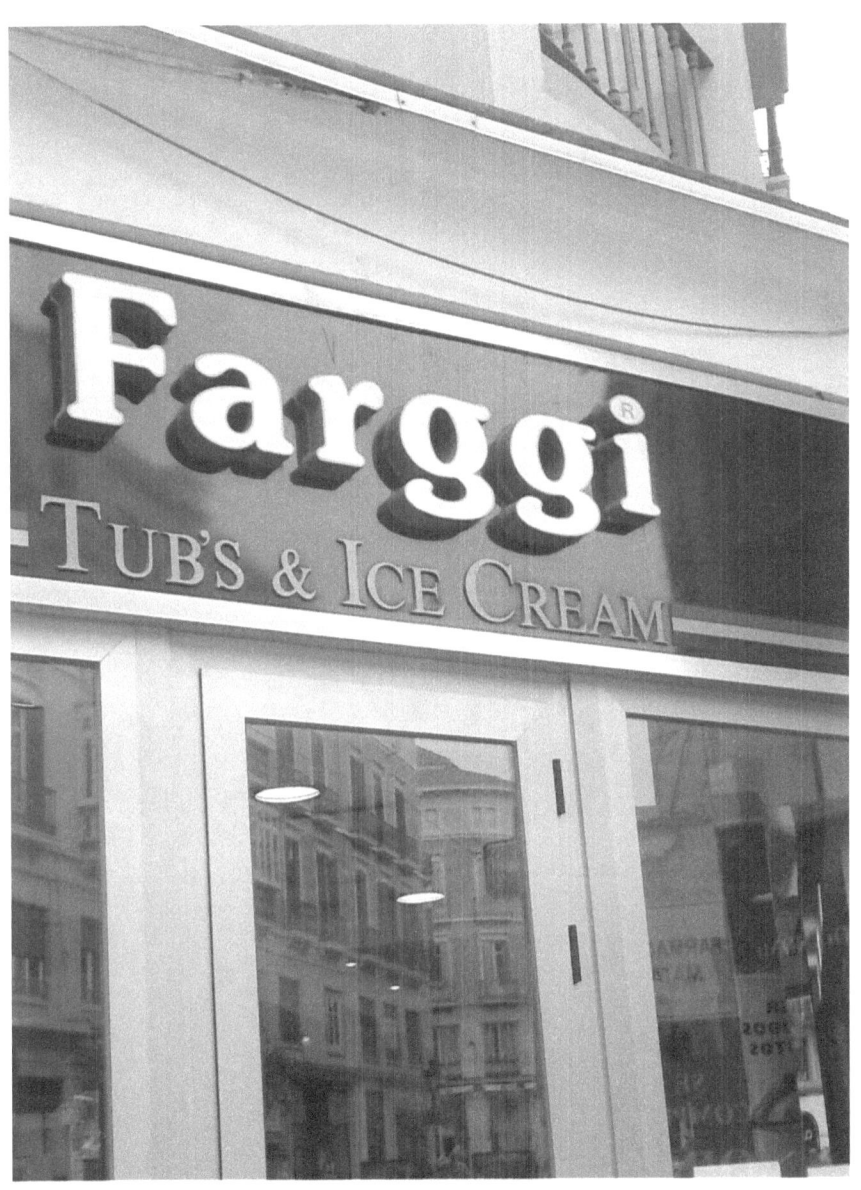

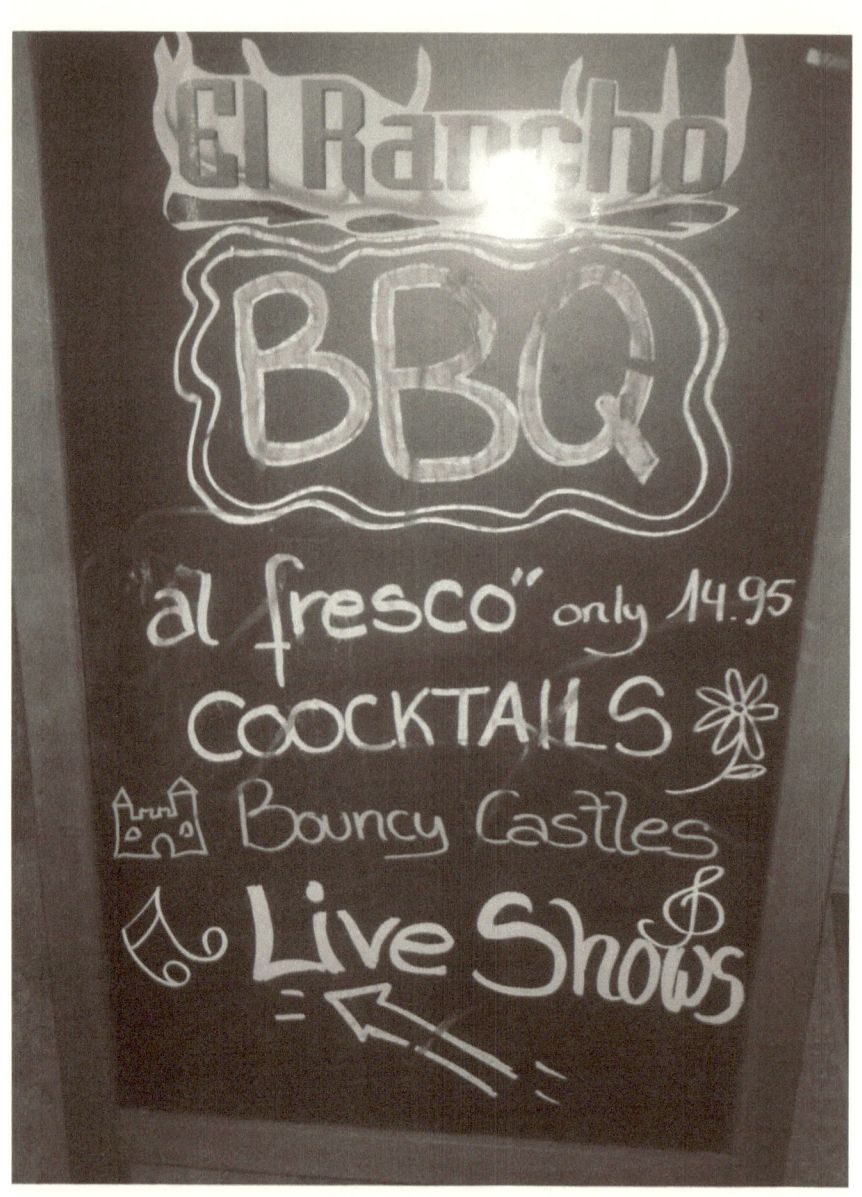

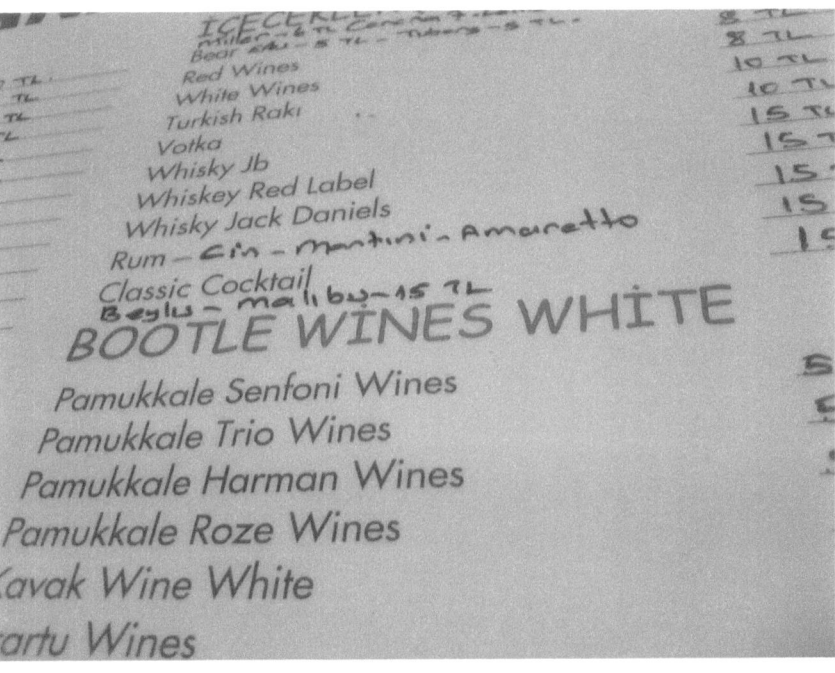

ICECLER...
Miller - ...6 TL Corona... Tuberg - 5 TL.
Bear #... 5 TL.
Red Wines
White Wines
Turkish Rakı
Votka
Whisky Jb
Whiskey Red Label
Whisky Jack Daniels
Rum – Gin – Martini – Amaretto
Classic Cocktail
Beylu – malibu – 15 TL

8 TL
8 TL
10 TL
10 TL
15 TL
15 T
15 :
15
19

BOOTLE WINES WHITE

Pamukkale Senfoni Wines

Pamukkale Trio Wines

Pamukkale Harman Wines

Pamukkale Roze Wines

Kavak Wine White

artu Wines

5

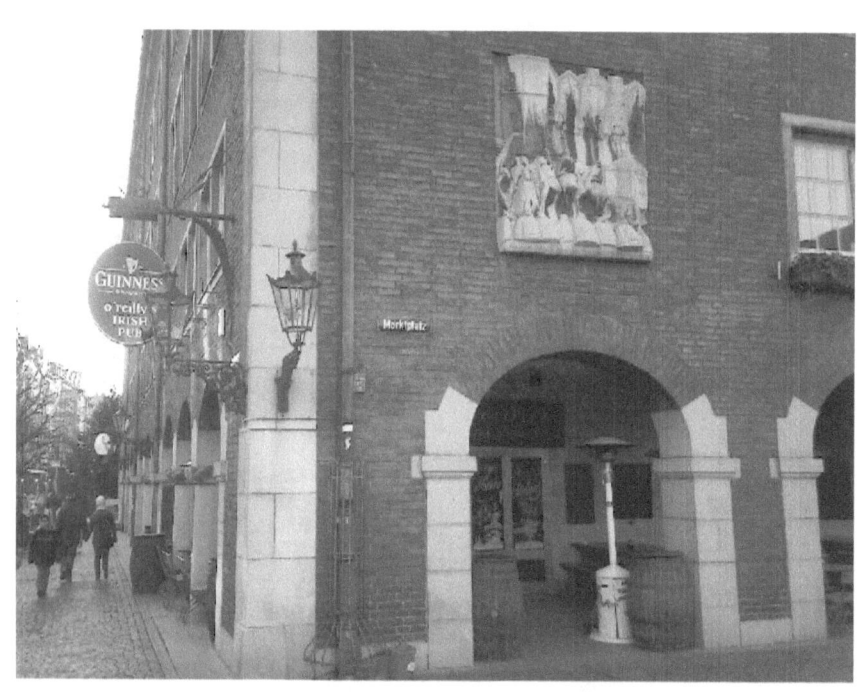

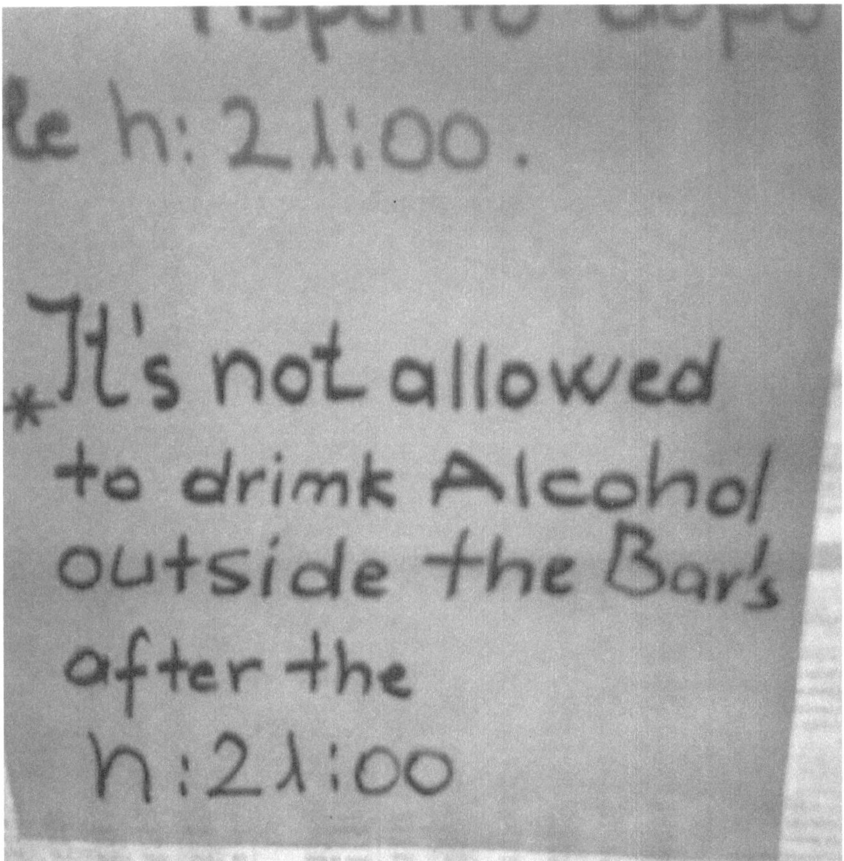

le h: 21:00 .

* It's not allowed
  to drimk Alcohol
  outside the Bar's
  after the
  h:21:00

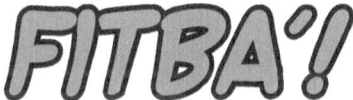

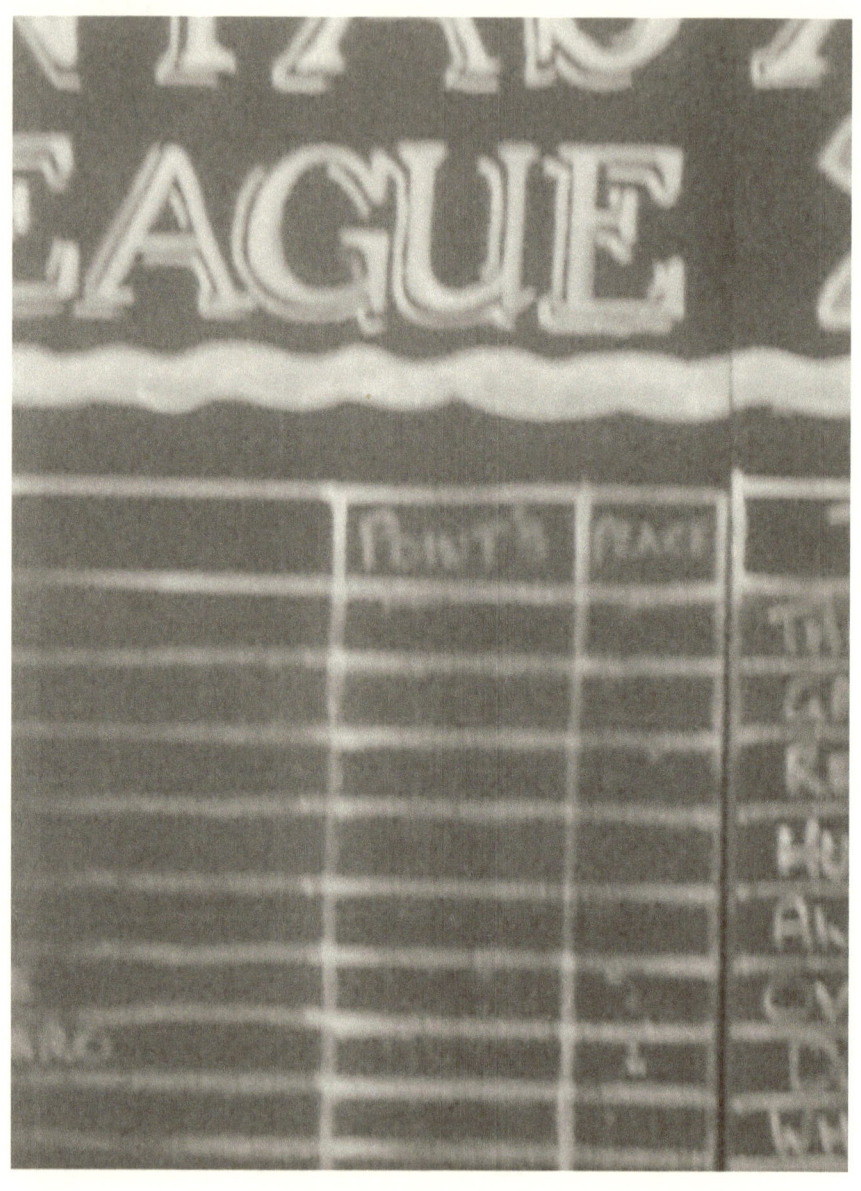

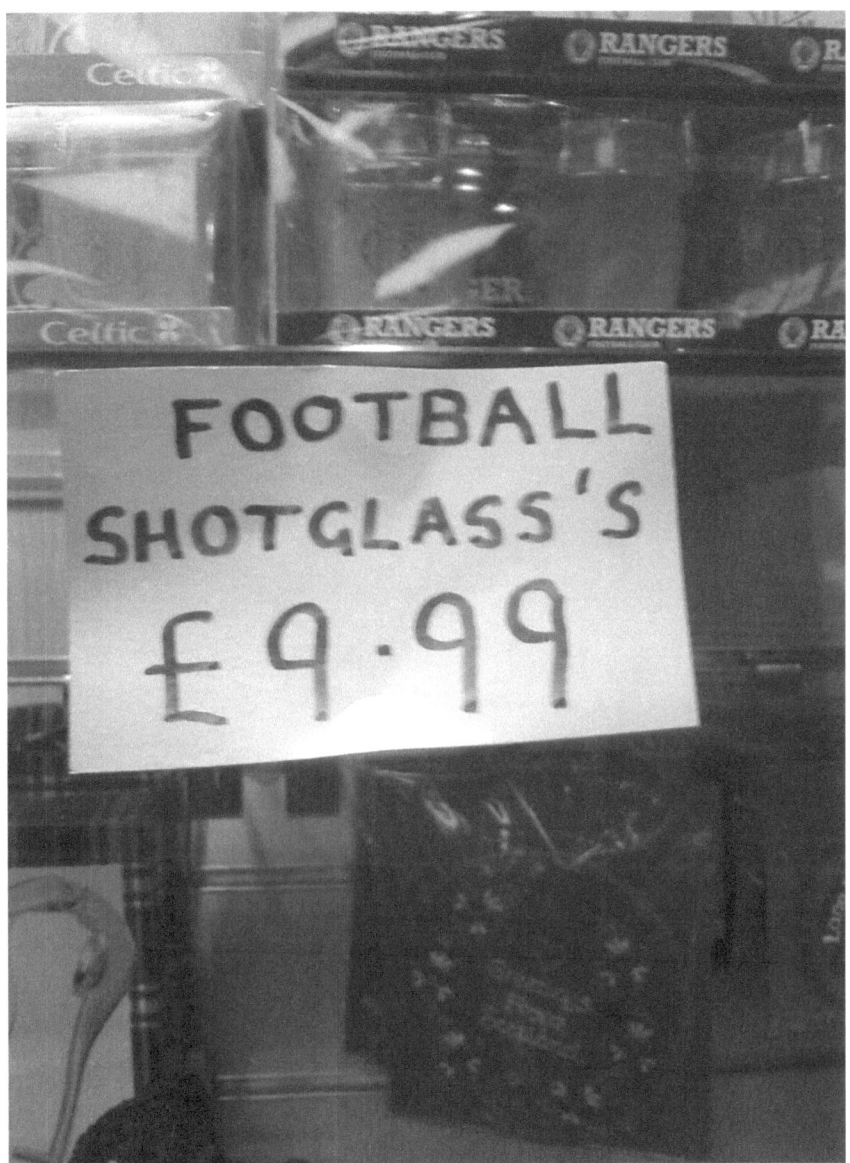

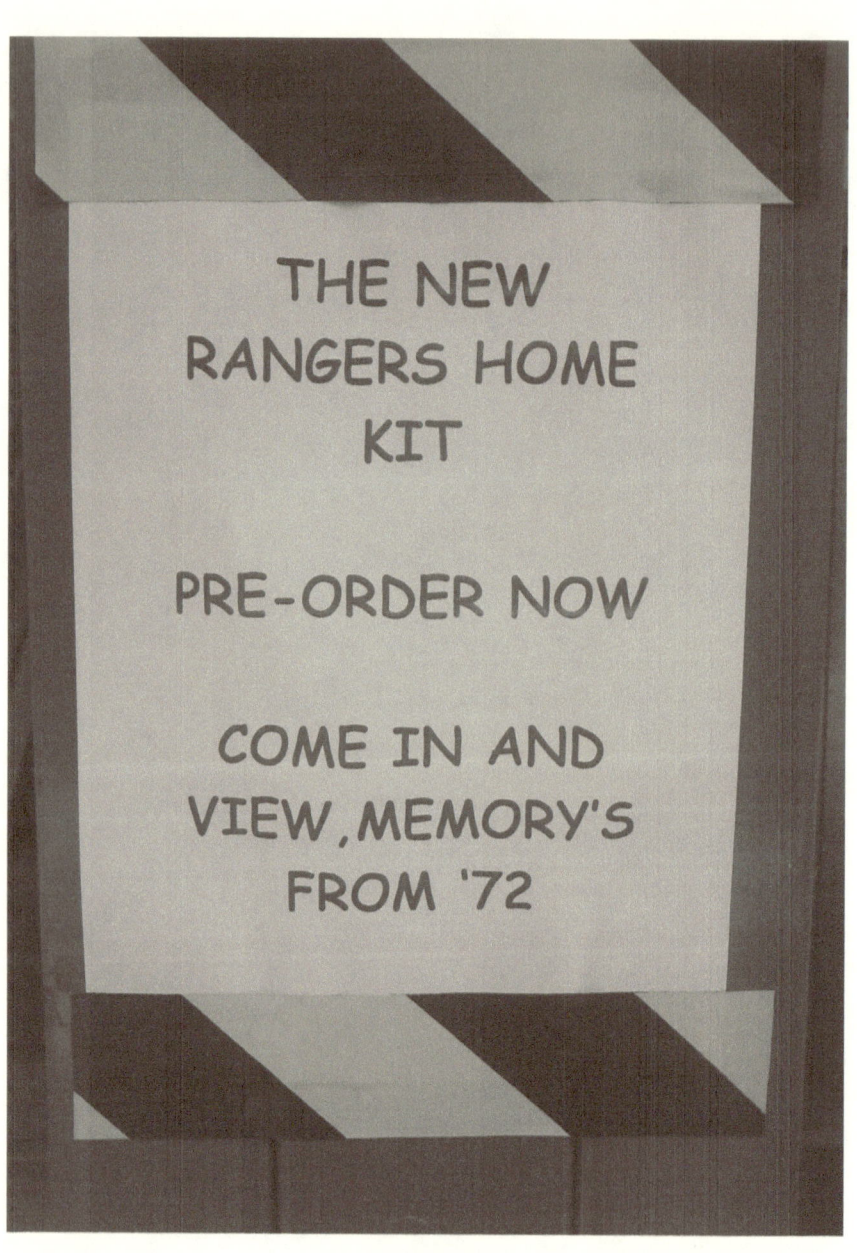

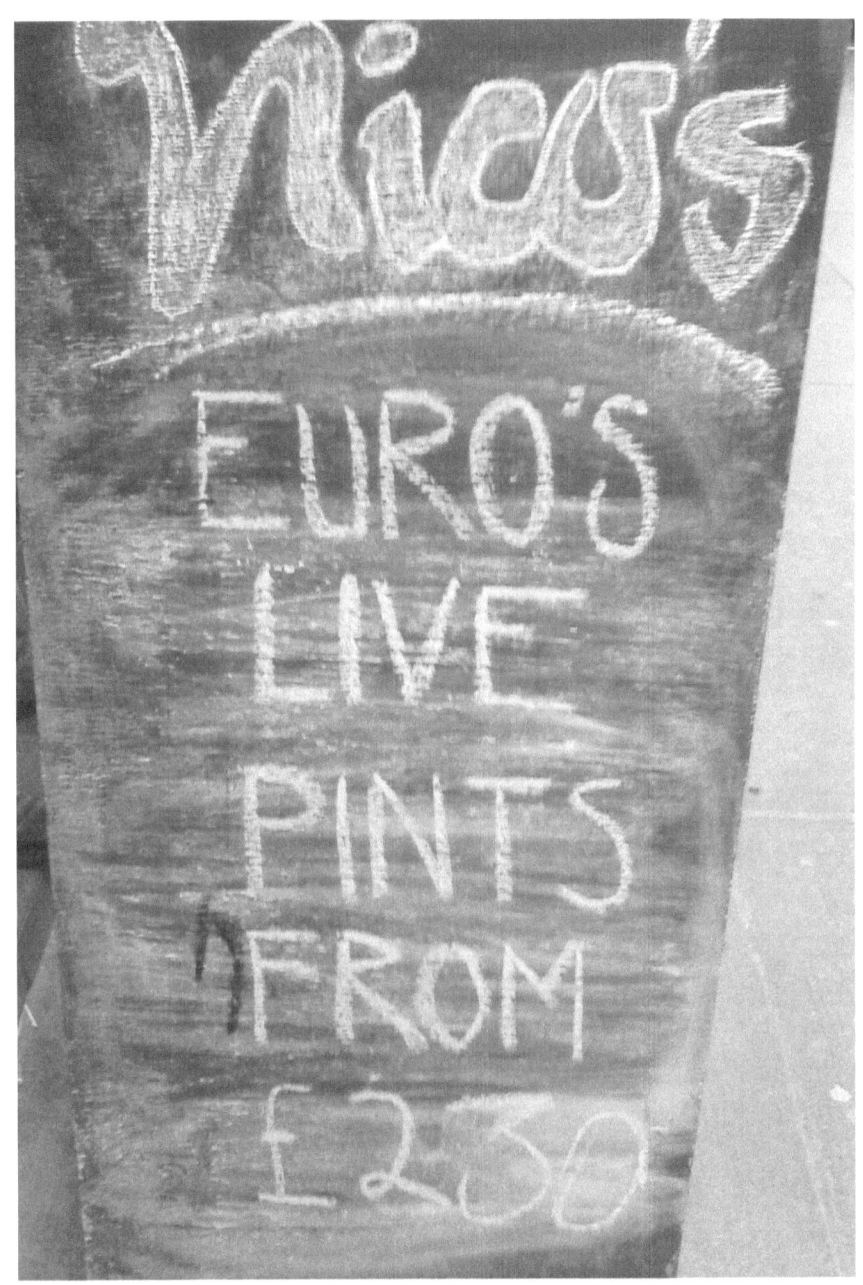

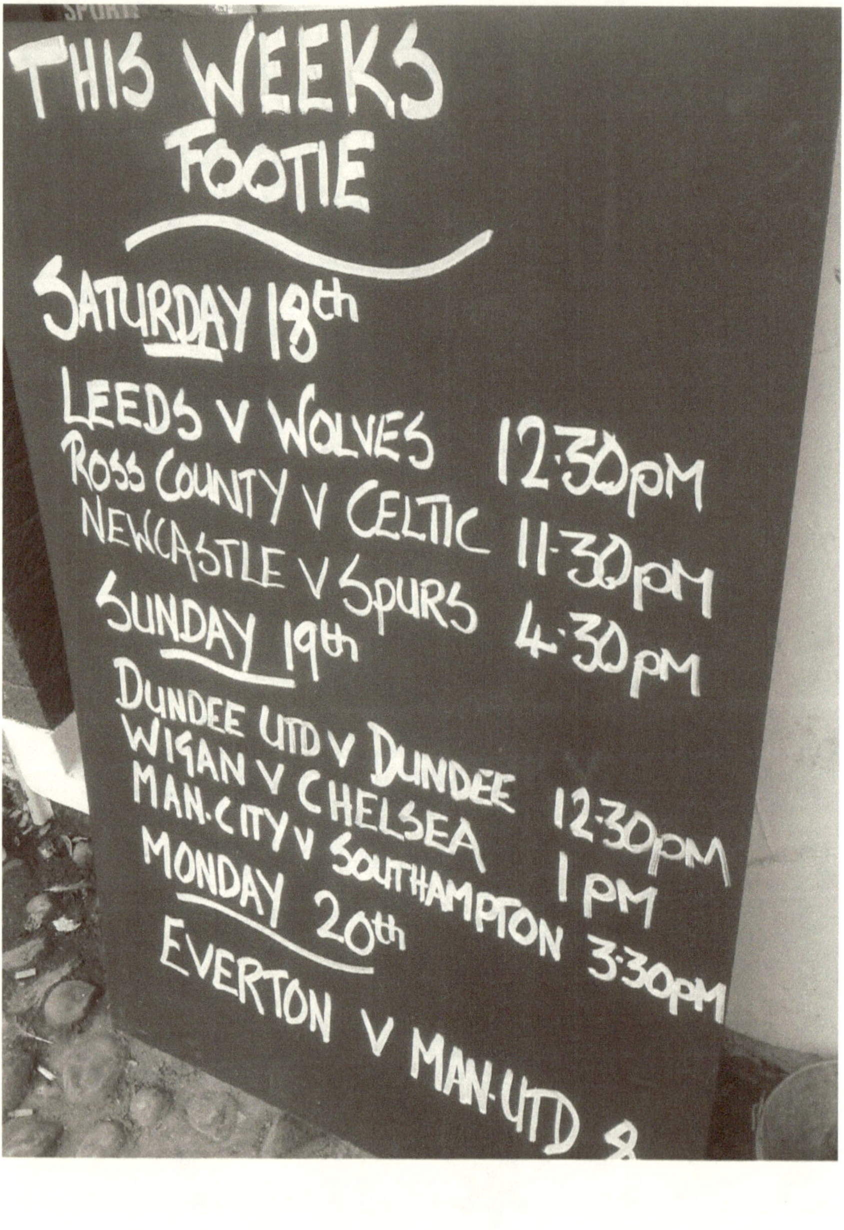
THIS WEEKS
FOOTIE
SATURDAY 18th
LEEDS V WOLVES 12:30PM
ROSS COUNTY V CELTIC 11:30PM
NEWCASTLE V SPURS 4:30PM
SUNDAY 19th
DUNDEE UTD V DUNDEE 12:30PM
WIGAN V CHELSEA 1PM
MAN.CITY V SOUTHAMPTON 3:30PM
MONDAY 20th
EVERTON V MAN-UTD

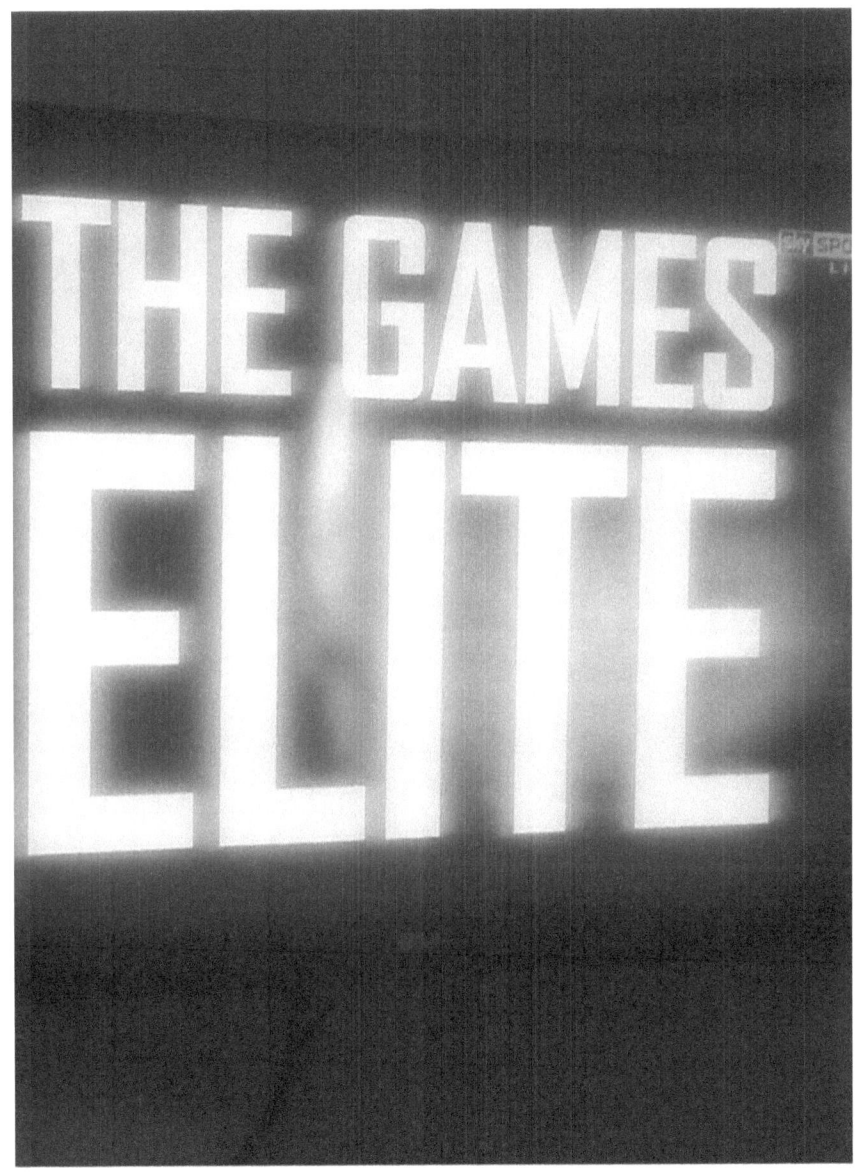

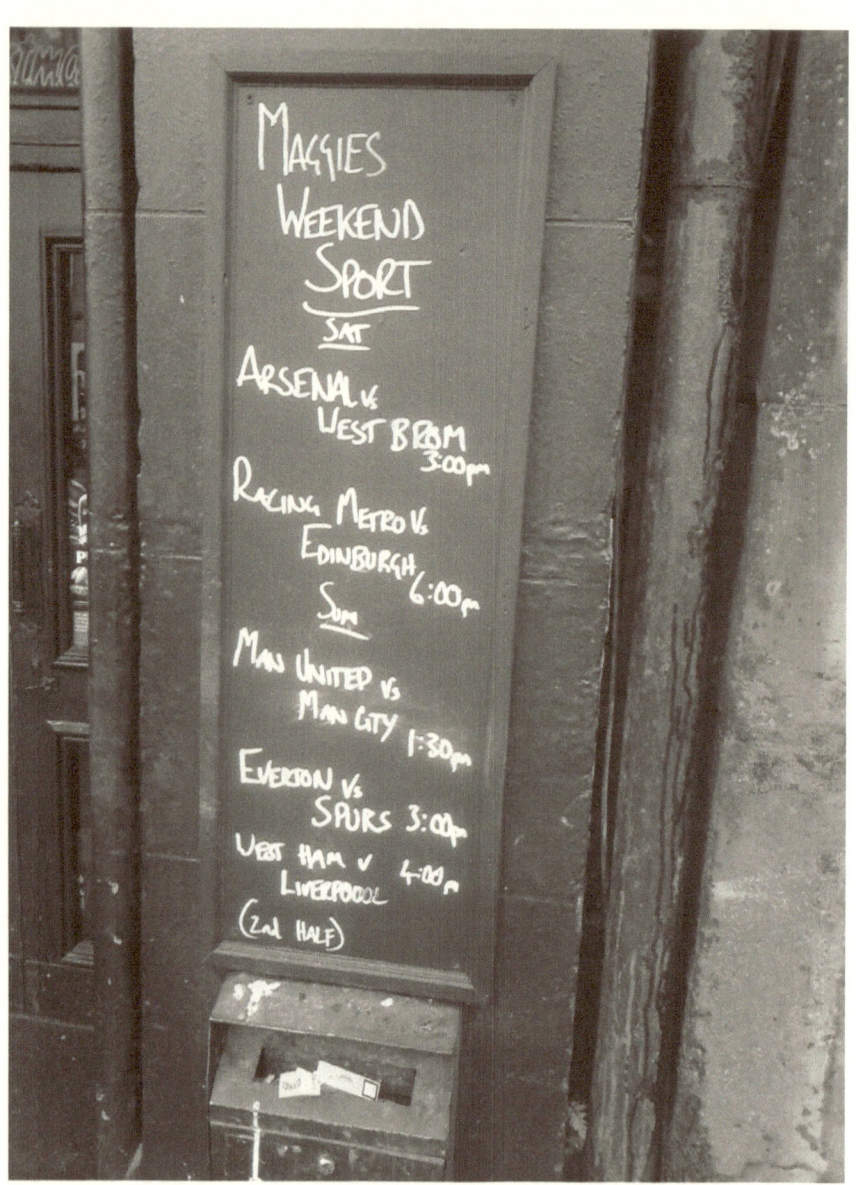

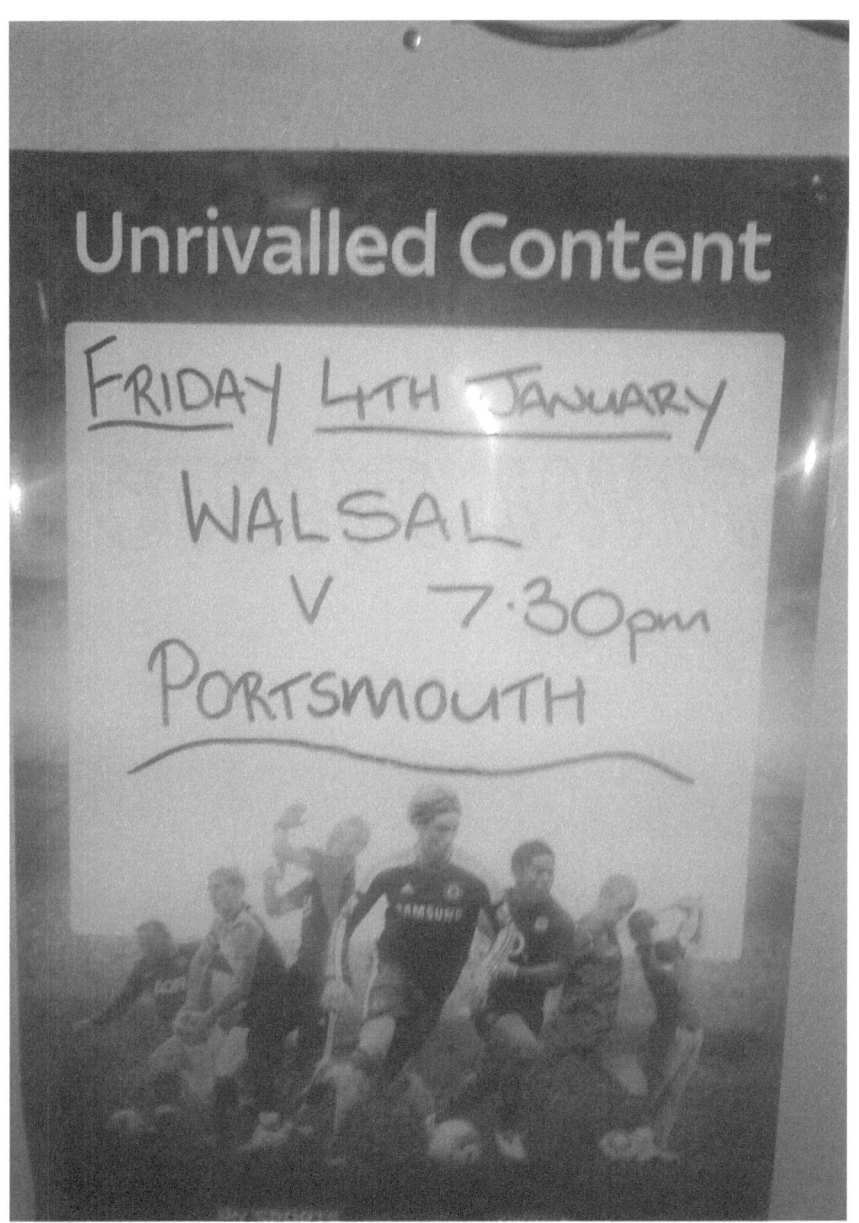

Unrivalled Content

FRIDAY 4TH JANUARY

WALSAL
V   7·30pm
PORTSMOUTH

FINAL PHOTO

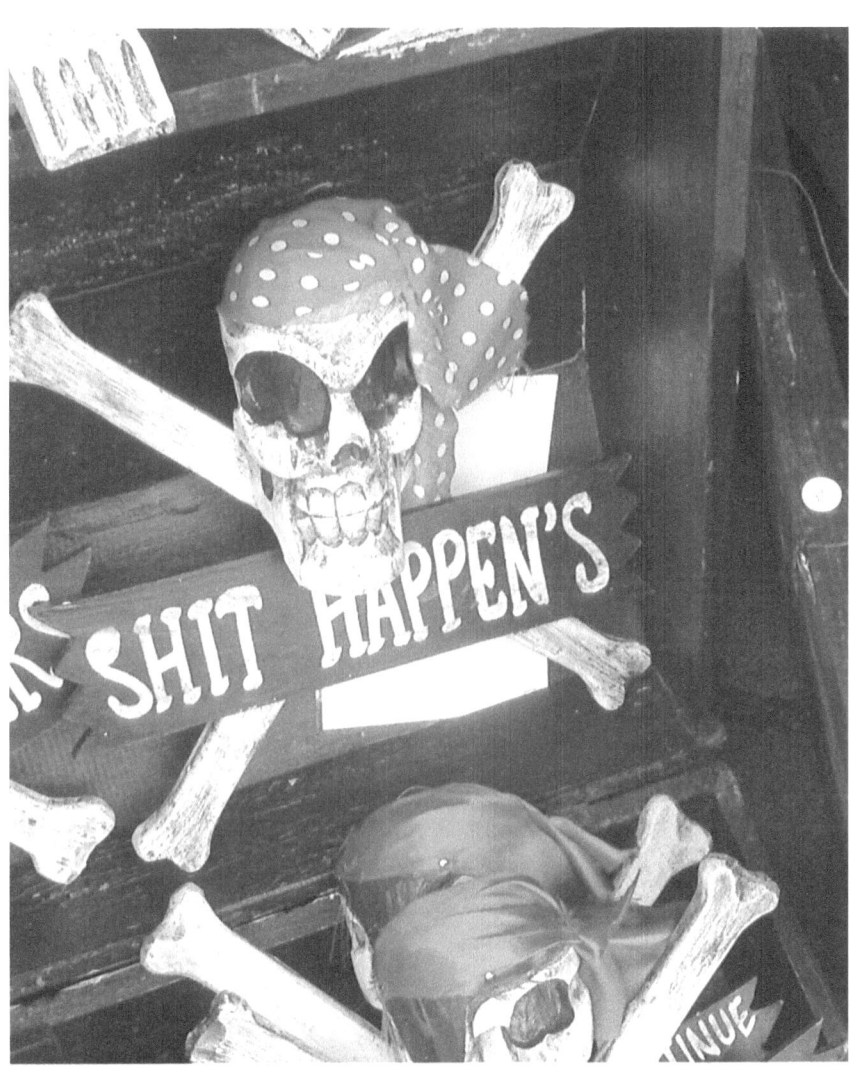

119

www.ingramcontent.com/pod-product-compliance
Lightning Source LLC
Chambersburg PA
CBHW030814180526
45163CB00003B/1288